PRAISE FOR PHOTOGRAPHY FOR WRITERS

"If you ever doubted your ability to take publishable pictures, this book will boost your confidence and change your mind. 'Photography for Writers' covers all the basics in simple language, peppered by Simon's usual touch of humour. A must for all writers keen to please editors and increase their income."

Solange Hando, *member of the British Guild of Travel Writers*

"Great book. I'm a writer but I'm not good at taking photographs. Simon's tips are excellent and it has given me confidence to submit photographs with my articles."

Natalie Roberts - five stars (Amazon)

"This a great little book that gives writers advice on how to add photography to their work and also make more money from having images to go with articles. Its something I have dabbled with and been surprised at how magazine editors especially will pay much more for your article when there are good quality photos to accompany it."

Sarah Watkins - five stars (Amazon)

PHOTOGRAPHY FOR WRITERS

HOW TO USE PHOTOS TO SELL MORE OF YOUR WORDS

SIMON WHALEY

© Simon Whaley

First published by Compass Books, 2014.

First edition ISBN: 978-1-78099-935-7

This second edition published by Simon Whaley, 2021.

Print ISBN: 978-1-8380786-0-7

eBook ISBN: 978-1-8380786-1-4

All rights reserved.

No part of this book may be reproduced in any form or by any electronic or mechanical means including information storage and retrieval systems, without written permission from the author, except for the use of brief quotations in a book review.

Enquiries concerning reproduction outside the scope of the above should be sent to the author, who can be contacted by email at *contact@simonwhaley.co.uk*.

V1/21

NEWSLETTER SIGN UP

If you'd like to stay up to date with my writing news and life from the Welsh Borders, visit the link below and you'll receive my occasional newsletter (and it will be occasional, because I'll be too busy writing other things to bombard you with regular newsletters!). And, it goes without saying, that under GDPR regulations, you'll be able to opt out at any time.

http://www.simonwhaley.co.uk/newsletter/

CONTENTS

NEWSLETTER SIGN UP	1
Foreword to the Second Edition	7
Introduction	9
1. WHY WRITERS SHOULD CONSIDER PHOTOGRAPHY	13
Letters & Fillers Market	15
Illustrated Articles	16
Step-by-Step Features	17
Non-Fiction Books	18
Research Material	19
The Digital Benefits	20
2. THE DIGITAL WORLD	23
Digital Camera Types	24
The Process of Capturing a Digital Image	28
Bring on the Buckets	29
Aperture	30
Shutter Speed	32
Sensitivity	34
Capturing a Photo	34
Understanding (Mega) Pixels	34
Print Resolution	36
Image Quality Settings	38
Digital File Types	38
3. TAKING PHOTOGRAPHS	41
Understanding Programme Modes	41
Play About	44
Planning the Images You Need	45
Light	48
Seek Out Unusual Angles	50
Photo Orientation - Landscape and Portrait	52
Understanding the Rule of Thirds	53

4. PHOTOGRAPHY LEGALITIES ... 59
Do You Need Permission? ... 59
Commercial Photography versus Editorial Photography ... 61
Release Forms ... 62
Copyright ... 64
Photographic Rights Offered ... 65
Watermarking ... 68

5. YOUR PERSONAL DIGITAL PHOTOGRAPHIC LIBRARY ... 71
Creating a Manageable Filing System ... 71
Cataloguing Software ... 73
Understanding Metadata and Keywording ... 75
Keywording ... 77
Adding Metadata Automatically ... 78
Basic Image Processing ... 78
Cloning ... 81
Image Manipulation ... 82
Backing Up Your Photos ... 83

6. MAGAZINES ... 87
Letters & Fillers ... 87
Fillers ... 88
Identifying the Opportunities for Writer-Photographers ... 91
Analysing Images used by a Magazine ... 93
Front Cover Images ... 97
Online Magazine Stores ... 98
Using Images to Secure a Commission ... 100
Using Someone Else's Photographs ... 101
Selecting the right Photos for your Articles ... 104
Step-by-Step Articles ... 105
Captions ... 106
Unique References ... 107
At the End of your Document ... 108
Never Insert Your Photos Into Your Text ... 108
Submitting your Images ... 109
Secondary Rights ... 111

7. NON-FICTION BOOKS 115
   Are Photos Necessary? 115
   Analysing the Market 116
   Plan the Images You Need 117
   Think Front Cover 121
   Captioning Images for Books 123
   List of Illustrations and Indexing Photos 123
   Self-Publishing 124

8. OTHER PHOTOGRAPHIC OPPORTUNITIES 127
   Photographic Agencies 127
   Tourist Brochures 130
   Greetings Cards 131
   Calendars 132
   Magazine Front Covers 133

9. PHOTOGRAPHY FOR RESEARCH 135
   Photography for Creative Writers 135
   Copying Research Material 137
   Using your Photographic Library for Idea Generation 141

10. THE FINAL EXPOSURE 145
    Understanding the Options 146
    Other Points to Consider 147
    Smile! 148

ENJOYED THE BOOK? 149

Also by Simon Whaley 151
About the Author 153

FOREWORD TO THE SECOND EDITION

The first edition of *Photography for Writers* was published back in 2014, when the only similar book for writers on this subject discussed 35mm colour transparencies and how to develop your negatives. By 2014, photography had changed considerably, and digital photography was putting a camera into everybody's pocket: the mobile phone.

Originally, I'd planned to include photographs in the book, as a way of illustrating some of the points I was making. However, to keep costs down, the publisher decided that an illustrated book was not cost-effective.

Like digital photography, publishing has evolved since 2014, to the extent that including images is now much easier and, thankfully, more cost-effective. So when the opportunity arose to update the book, I decided I was only going to do so if I could include some photographs.

Photography has also evolved since 2014. Apple launched the iPhone 6 with an 8-megapixel camera and Samsung's Galaxy Alpha came with a 12-megapixel camera. At that time I was also using a Canon 5D Mark II digital SLR camera.

The latest iPhone now has not one, but three lenses, each with 12 megapixels, while the latest Samsung phone comes with a 48-megapixel camera. My large digital SLR camera has been replaced by the smaller, mirrorless Fuji XT2.

However, this book is not about having the latest photographic technology. Most writers can't afford it. (I'd love the latest Fuji mirrorless camera!) More importantly, most writers don't *need* the latest technology.

All we need is a little guidance on how to take a publishable image and then use it to sell more of our words.

I'm immensely grateful for the reviews the first edition had. I hope this second edition helps you. Please do leave a review, and get in touch with me (contact@simonwhaley.co.uk) to let me know about your successes.

Simon Whaley,

June 2020

INTRODUCTION

I sold a 1200-word article to an American magazine for £200 ($250). They also used six of my photographs, for which they paid me an additional £600 ($740). So, which would you rather be: the writer who gets £200 ($250) or the writer/photographer who gets £900 ($1100)?

To the uninitiated, photography may seem as though it's all about shutter speeds, apertures, and interchangeable lenses. For serious photographers it still is. However, the advent of digital photography has enabled *anyone* and *everyone* to take a decent, publishable photograph. That includes you: the freelance writer. Armed with a simple digital camera, you too could become the writer/photographer earning extra cash. In the right market, even an image captured on a mobile phone is publishable and can earn you some money.

Pick up any magazine from a newsagent's shelf, flick through the pages, and you can't fail to notice how visual today's publications are. Whether it's a letter on a magazine's letters page, a filler on a household tips page, or an article, photographs are everywhere. Even illustrated non-fiction books are cheaper to produce these days.

To get your photos published alongside your words you do not need to be a professional photographer with six different camera bodies, 22 different interchangeable lenses and a photographic exhibition running in a top London gallery. All you need is a digital camera. It can be one of those compact cameras you buy from any high street store and slip into your pocket. Or it could be your mobile phone. And it's not necessary to do lots of processing with the image on your computer afterwards either. If you can hold a camera steady and press a button, you can take a publishable photo, capable of illustrating your words.

That's not to say that professional photographers are wasting their time; they're not. With the right equipment, software and knowledge they can take fantastically stunning photos. My interest in photography has developed (no pun intended) so much, I now use a camera many professionals use. This means I spend time processing my photos in what many photographers have come to call 'the digital darkroom' (using computer software). But this book will show you that you don't need a professional camera, or complicated software, to take publishable photographs to accompany your words.

As a creative writing tutor and workshop facilitator, I'm regularly asked how to submit photos with articles and books. Do you insert them into your text, or send them as separate attachments? Do you email them, or send a link to a folder in the cloud somewhere? What does hi-res mean and why do magazines want photos at 300dpi? What is 300dpi? All of these questions, and many more, will be answered in *Photography for Writers*.

Photography for Writers will show you:

• how to take pictures that an editor will want to use,

- what picture quality is about, and why images from the Internet are useless (and why using them may be illegal),

- how to use your camera effectively, to get better images (without getting technical),

- how to file and store your photos,

- how to use someone else's photographs, for free, (and legally) to illustrate your articles,

- how to submit an illustrated article to a publication,

- the legalities of where and when you can and can't take photos for publication.

There's even advice about how to take your photography a little further, opening up new markets, to enable you to make the most of the photos you've already taken. And there are useful tips and advice about how to use your camera as a research tool.

I also believe that writers should be photographers for another reason. We're observers. We watch and notice things and jot down those thoughts. When you look at the world with a photographer's eye, you'll notice even more, and for a writer that's great! Having a camera with you at all times to capture any interesting scenes and images can generate more ideas.

Photography for Writers will show that by offering photos with your words you can increase the amount of money you are paid for your ideas, open up new markets you may never have considered before, and demystify the process of submitting your images. If everything about taking publishable photos has been a blur to you, *Photography for Writers* will bring it all sharply into focus. (And that pun was intended!)

1

WHY WRITERS SHOULD CONSIDER PHOTOGRAPHY

Take a look at any magazine and you'll see that it is full of glossy, colourful pictures. Some magazines have more photographs than words. If you aspire to be a freelance writer and want to sell your words to a magazine, or if you've had some success to date but want to build upon that success, then I believe you should consider adding photography to your list of skills. Why? Because it makes good business sense.

A freelance writer is a business looking for customers: magazines or publishers. Magazines and publishers are looking for suppliers: freelance writers and freelance photographers. Now, think about this relationship from an editor's perspective. If a freelance writer submits an article called *How To Forage For Food* and the editor likes it, the editor has two options:

- To look for suitable photos from a photographic agency or some other picture source,
- To hire a freelance photographer to go out and take some suitable images.

What happens if the editor's photographic budget doesn't cover the fee the photographic agency requires for the photos the editor wants to use? That time searching for suitable images has been wasted. Commissioning a freelance photographer to take some photographs takes time too. What happens if the freelance photographer doesn't provide the exact photos the editor was looking for, or the weather wasn't right on the day? That's more time wasted. Time editors don't have. (Who does?)

I spent many years writing a regular column for a county magazine, and during a meeting with the editor, she said:

> *"My dream supplier is someone who can provide the words and pictures. Every page in my magazine needs a words-and-picture package because every page is illustrated with photos. If a writer sends me an article I want to use, but it doesn't have any photos, I then have to spend time trying to find suitable images. At particularly busy times, if I have a page to fill and I have a choice between a well-written article without pictures or a good article that needs some editing but comes with photographs, I will always go with the good article with pictures. As an editor, my skill is editing text. I can edit a good article into a great article in a couple of minutes. Finding the right photographs can take two or three hours."*

There you have it. Straight from the horse's mouth. (Not that the editor looked anything like a horse, I hasten to add.) Writers who can provide editors with a complete words-and-picture package are making the editor's life easier. So why shouldn't that writer be you? If you have a camera go and dig it out from the back of the cupboard because soon it's going to be earning you some cash. And if you don't have a camera, consider investing in one because you could recover its cost with your first sale.

Letters & Fillers Market

Magazines love reader-interactivity, and a great way to do this is to invite readers to send in letters where they can comment on articles they've read in previous issues, or simply share something that has happened in their own lives. In many magazines, the readers' letter page often has a club-like feel to it, as if they are friends gathering together to share news over a coffee. Photographs, nowadays, accompany many of these letters, and some magazines will pay extra for those letters with photos.

Many of the better paying opportunities are in the women's weekly magazines, so here's an example of some of the words-and-picture opportunities I've found in one issue of one such magazine:

- The Readers' Letter Page - every letter is accompanied by a photograph. The photograph is often a humorous one with the reader in a funny situation, or perhaps a reader's child in a cute pose. The magazine paid these readers £100 ($120) for every piece used. This is where you need to understand that if you want your letter published in this section then you must include a photograph too.
- Readers' Top Tips Page - This page has 12 useful household tips, sent in by readers. Seven have photographs accompanying them, five are words only. The magazine paid £30 ($35) for word-only tips, but £60 ($75) for tips accompanied by a photograph. See? Supplying photos means the earning potential is greater.

- Readers' Special Moments - a double-page spread where readers share those special days in their lives: marriages, anniversaries, thrilling holidays or fun days out. Every story has a photograph, for which the magazine paid £40 ($50). So, no photograph means you don't stand a chance of selling your words to this slot.
- Another letters page is devoted to the silly things in life. Again, every letter is illustrated with a photograph and they paid £100 ($125) for the Letter of the Week, and £50 ($60) for all of the other letters used, plus another £25 ($30) for every photograph used.

None of the photographs on these pages has been taken by professional photographers in a photographic studio. They've all been taken by the readers on their mobile phones, or possibly with a small compact camera. Many are the type of photos share with family and friends on Facebook, Twitter and Instagram. They're just ordinary photos, but they're earning the writer extra money.

Illustrated Articles

A writer who provides illustrated articles can improve their fortunes in two ways:

- Some magazines will pay extra for the photographs, in addition to the words. Sometimes, this extra money can make writing the article worth the effort in the first place. For example, one magazine used to pay £30 ($35) for 1,000 words, which isn't much! This is not a market I would normally consider. However, they also paid £25 ($30) for every photograph published and they often used eight images per

article. Whilst a 1,000-word article would earn the writer £30 ($35), a 1,000-word illustrated article would earn £230 ($280). Being able to offer photographs can turn a poor market into a useful market worth writing for.
- Some magazines won't pay extra for photographs, but they only accept complete words-and-picture packages. Therefore, being able to provide photos opens up these new markets to you. Who doesn't want more customers? And while they don't pay anything extra for photographs, their rates of pay tend to be higher than those markets that will just buy the words from you. So that mobile phone in your pocket could be the key to new magazine markets.

Illustrated articles are more interesting to the reader. Often, it is the photographs that grab the reader's interest first, as they flick through the pages. Those images complement the words, while also adding extra detail. A travel feature needs photographs showing readers the locations and attractions that can be experienced at these destinations. A cookery magazine needs a photograph of the finished dish to accompany the recipe. A gardening article needs photographs to show the different plants and flowers used in a design. Look at any article in any magazine and imagine the photos were not there. Suddenly, the page looks drab and boring.

Step-by-Step Features

Have you ever followed a step-by-step article? Photographs are used to explain a technical aspect of the process, or to show the reader what something should look like before they move onto the next stage. Photographs give the readers confidence that they are following the instructions properly. They do not need to be stunningly beautiful images, worthy of a posh art gallery; they simply need to be in focus and show a specific aspect of the project.

While step-by-step features are popular in certain types of magazines (particularly craft, DIY and gardening titles), they can appear anywhere, if you have the right idea. I sold an article showing readers how to clean up their garden fishpond in ten easy steps. One of the photographs used was of a dirty pile of slimy sludge that I'd cleared out from the bottom of the garden pond. It certainly wasn't a beautiful image, but it illustrated the step in the article, which is why the magazine bought it. The feature was 800-words long and had twelve photos. They paid £100 ($125) for the words and another £240 ($300) for the photographs.

Without photographs, a writer will have difficulty selling a step-by-step feature because editors can't get the photos from anywhere else unless they commission a photographer to tackle the step-by-step process and take the photos. If you're going to create a step-by-step article, you might as well take the photographs yourself.

Non-Fiction Books

When you've sold several articles on one particular topic, you might want to think about turning the information in those features into a book. Publishers look more favourably on writers whose work has already been published in magazine format, so if your camera has opened up new magazine markets, it could also lead to bigger projects, such as non-fiction books.

One of my markets is providing walking route descriptions for some of the walking magazines, and this includes supplying photographs of the views and interesting sights walkers can see on route. I had an idea for a walking book and approached a publisher with a proposal. Having studied the publisher's series I was targeting, I noticed all of their books in this particular series had two photographs per walking route. So I made a point in my book proposal that I could supply a selection of photographs, enabling them to select at least two for each route.

I also included photocopies of my published walking routes, all of which included photographs. This gave the publishers an idea of the photos I could provide, whilst also demonstrating that I was used to taking photographs to complement my words. The book was commissioned and during a conversation the publisher advised me that had they needed to source the images from elsewhere, the cost would have to have been deducted from *my* advance. So, not only did photos help me to secure the contract, but they also saved me money.

Research Material

As writers, we're forever being told to carry a notebook and pen with us at all times to jot down ideas as they come to us. (I guarantee you will forget an idea if you don't write it down.) However, in addition to a notebook and pen, every writer should also carry a camera at all times. These days, that's easy; most mobile phones have built- in cameras, and few of us seem capable of going anywhere without our phones.

Cameras make fantastic research tools. Think of them as pictorial notebooks. Want to make a note of the castle you're visiting? Does it have a drawbridge? How many arrow slots are in each tower? What colour are the stone walls? All you need to do is take a few photographs and you'll be able to answer all of these questions at any time in the future. Photographs are capable of triggering memories, which is why cameras make brilliant research tools. Take a photo of a fish and chip shop on the coast and your nostrils will soon be twitching at the smell of vinegar on hot, fluffy, just-out-of-the-frier chips. (Go on, admit it. You can smell them right now, can't you?)

The Digital Benefits

Digital photography has many benefits:

- Instantaneous. Take a photo on a digital camera and it's on the LCD screen within seconds. This means that when you take a photo, if it doesn't look right, you can delete it and take another, better photo.
- Cost. Digital photos are much cheaper than the rolls of film that used to contain 24 or 36 frames. Film forced photographers to think carefully about capturing the photo in the first place. That's not to say that we can be slapdash with the composition of our photos; we can't. For professional photographers, thinking carefully about composition is vital, but digital cameras allow us to experiment to find the right composition we're looking for, at no extra cost. All we're limited by is the size of our memory card (which is capable of holding hundreds, if not thousands, of photographs). That's brilliant for photos we want to take for research purposes. But it also offers flexibility. I often take two photos of a scene: one with the camera held horizontally (often called landscape) and one with the camera rotated vertically (known as portrait). A landscape photo might be used in a magazine as a double-page spread (across two pages), whilst a portrait photo might be used on one page, or even the front cover of the magazine. Digital means that taking two photos of the same scene doesn't cost anything extra (except

some space on your memory card or computer hard drive).
- Copies. With digital, it is easier making copies. Download the photos to your computer and then back them up to another disk in case your main computer fails. This also means when you send photos to editors, you send them a copy, not the original. With film, you either sent the original, or you paid extra to get another copy made.

So, as you can see, every writer with a camera has more opportunities to sell their words, which increases the amount of money they can earn as a freelance writer. The only outlay is at the start when you buy the camera and a couple of memory cards. If you're serious about your writing, these items are tax-deductible. They are legitimate business expenses that you can claim against any profits you make from your writing. Find some good markets, though, and you'll find the camera repays itself many, many times over.

2

THE DIGITAL WORLD

Cameras work by capturing the light that passes through a lens. Pre-digital cameras caught the light on film, which users then had to send off to be processed, or they took it to a developer on the high street. Digital cameras capture the light via a sensor, which converts the image into digital data that can be stored on a memory card. These memory cards are relatively cheap, and they are capable of storing hundreds, if not thousands of images.

A huge benefit of digital cameras is that they display this digital data on an in-built screen as soon as it has been taken. This means you can assess the shot quickly. So, if you were taking a photo of the beach-side hotel you are staying at and then noticed your image has a dustcart running along the road outside, you can delete it and take another photo. Imagine your dismay if you'd been using film and not noticed the dustcart in the shot until you were back home when your photos had been processed.

Another benefit of digital cameras is that the number of pictures you can take is dictated (mainly) by the capacity of the memory card you are using. The memory card on my digital camera enables me to store nearly 600 photos. When using film, I could only manage 36 shots on a single roll of film.

Film was quite expensive to process and, because there were only 36 shots on each roll, I was always making a judgement about whether to take a photograph or not. With digital cameras you can take as many photos as you like; subject to how much room you have on your memory card, or how many memory cards you have with you. Once you have your camera and memory card, it doesn't cost any more money to process your images on your computer (except for the electricity to run your computer). That's why digital cameras can be great research tools for writers; you can take as many images as you need to remind yourself about a place, or event.

Digital Camera Types

If you don't already have a digital camera, or perhaps you're thinking of upgrading your existing model, here's a breakdown of the main types of digital cameras and what they will enable you to do.

Compact: A compact camera slips into a pocket easily. Prices start from £25 ($30) and can go higher than £300 ($360). Most are simple to use, merely requiring you to point the camera at what you want to take a photograph of and then press a button to capture the image. This is why they're sometimes called point-and-shoot cameras. (Some photographers claim *every* camera is a point-and-shoot camera because point-and-shoot is an attitude of mind. It describes the photographer, not the camera.)

With compact cameras, the camera does it all for you. In automatic mode, it takes a useful image, most of the time.

They also have a range of other modes, or programme settings, to help capture certain types of photos (which we'll look at in more detail in Chapter 3).

Compact cameras have one lens, and, usually, this is a zoom lens, allowing you to get closer to what you want to take a photograph of without having to physically move closer to the object. How far you can zoom is one of the factors that determines a compact camera's price. However, the more zoom capability a camera has, the more flexibility it offers. (Some cameras have an *optical zoom* and/or a *digital zoom*. The optical zoom refers to the actual lens: how far it can zoom in on a subject. The digital zoom is some built-in computer wizardry that enlarges the image to make it look bigger. In reality, this enlargement can lead to some distortion or blurring of the image. So if you're buying a camera and comparing different models, concentrate on the optical zoom rather than the digital zoom.)

The other major influence on a compact camera's price is the number of megapixels the sensor has. This determines picture quality and size (I'll explain this in more detail in this chapter). Generally, a compact camera with more than 8 megapixels will usually provide good, publishable images.

Single-Lens Reflex (SLR): A single-lens reflex camera is what many professional photographers use. This camera comes in two parts: the body and the lens, which means that you can change the lens. Each lens has its speciality, so the number and type of lenses a photographer has will depend upon the type of photography they enjoy.

These models are bulkier than compact cameras, which means they're heavier and more difficult to carry. They are also more expensive, with the latest bottom-of-the-range models starting from around £500 ($610), extending to the top-of-the-range models which cost over £3,000 ($3,600) ...

and sometimes that's just the body; that doesn't include any lenses.

Whilst many of these cameras have an automatic mode, that's not what they are bought for. Photographers buy these cameras so they can set all of the different variables, like shutter speeds, apertures, and the light sensitivity of the sensor. These cameras allow the photographer to have much more artistic control over the images that they capture.

Prosumer (also known as Bridge cameras): These cameras are a cross between the professional SLR cameras and the consumer-friendly compact cameras. They're sometimes known as Bridge cameras because they bridge the gap between professional and consumer cameras. This sector of the market changes quickly. Traditionally, prosumer cameras are shaped like an SLR camera, but they don't have interchangeable lenses. Instead, they have one long zoom lens like many of the compact cameras, but they also enable photographers to set apertures and shutter speeds. Prices for these products range from £200 ($250) up to £600 ($740). People who want to develop their photographic interests further, sometimes buy one of these cameras, before progressing to a single-lens reflex camera.

Mirrorless (sometimes called Compact System Cameras): There's been a huge growth in mirrorless cameras. The professional SLR camera has a mirror in it. This reflects the image captured through the lens up to the viewfinder. When the photograph is taken, the mirror flips out of the way so the light through the lens hits the sensor behind. Making room for the mirror to flip out of the way is part of the reason why single-lens reflex cameras are bigger.

However, these mirrorless cameras, as their name implies, don't have mirrors, so they don't need the space for a mirror to flip out of the way. They often have an electronic viewfinder, which displays what the sensor is seeing. As a result, these are not much bigger than a compact camera, but have interchangeable lenses, making them ideal for people who travel. Indeed, this is the system that I have switched to. I traded in my digital SLR for one of these, and it's so much lighter to carry around. And it has other benefits too - because it's lighter, I get less camera shake when I'm hand-holding my camera, resulting in fewer blurred photos. Some of these mirrorless cameras now have image stabilisers built-in, reducing the risk of blurred images even further. Prices start from around £800 ($975) and can go into the thousands.

Mobile Phones: The quality of mobile phone cameras is improving all of the time. Many have sensors with the same number of megapixels as some compact cameras. However, the sensor quality isn't as good as those sensors in the mirrorless or SLR cameras. It's like comparing apples and oranges. They're both fruit, but with different qualities.

A mobile phone camera will take photos capable of being printed in a magazine or book. In the first edition of this book, I suggested that images taken on a mobile phone were acceptable when using them at a relatively small size: perhaps on a readers' letter page, or as a small image (say 6 x 4 inches) to illustrate an article. But technology is improving all of the time. In fact, in September 2017, *TIME* magazine produced twelve different front covers that had all been taken on an Apple iPhone. That's how good mobile phone cameras are these days.

And, of course, mobile phone cameras are perfect for taking research images.

So, you may find that your mobile phone camera is perfect for your needs. There's a saying many photographers use:

"The best camera is the one you have in your hand."

It's better to have any sort of camera with you, rather than no camera at all and miss the opportunity to take a photo!

The Process of Capturing a Digital Image

I know when I take a photo, I take one in my head first. No, I don't have a bionic eye. (Actually, I have a bit of a wonky eye after experiencing a detached retina, but that's another story.)

What I mean is, when I see a scene, I often picture in my mind what the photograph will look like, before I've taken it. Our disappointment with our images often comes when the image we capture is not the one that we imagined it to be.

You don't need to understand everything the camera is doing when you press the shutter button and take a photo, but if you can grasp the basics, you'll get much more out of your digital camera. And you're more likely to capture images that look like you how you imagined they would.

Compact, bridge, mirrorless and even SLR cameras have many programme modes for capturing different types of photos (landscapes, sporting events, close-ups). Indeed, your mobile phone may even offer a choice of modes. So, once you understand what the camera is doing when it takes a photo using one of these modes, it will help you to select the right mode.

When we take a photograph, light flows through the lens of the camera and hits the sensor. Two things affect how much of this light reaches our camera's sensor: aperture and shutter speed.

Aperture: This influences how *much* light reaches the camera's sensor. Imagine a barrier in the lens of the camera that has a hole in the centre. This hole can be made bigger, to allow more light in, or smaller to reduce the amount of light reaching the sensor.

Shutter Speed: This determines how *long* that amount of light flows through the hole, onto the sensor.

It's the different combinations of how those two functions work together that gives us this variety of modes.

Bring on the Buckets

Take an empty bucket, and place a plastic sheet with a 10 cm (4 in) hole in the middle over the top of it. Pick up a watering can and pour water over the top of the bucket for ten seconds. The amount of water you capture in your bucket has been affected by the sheet of plastic with the hole in it, and also by the ten-second period you were pouring in the water.

In this example, the sheet of plastic with the hole represented the camera's aperture, and the ten-second pouring of water represented the shutter speed. If you were to replace the plastic sheet with one that has a 20 cm (8 in) hole (and emptied the bucket of any water) and then poured water from the watering can for the same ten-second period, your bucket will have captured much more water. Although the water-pouring length of time was the same (our shutter speed), the hole (our aperture) was much bigger, and so more water was captured by the bucket.

If we emptied the bucket again, replaced the plastic sheet with the 20 cm (8 in) hole and then poured in water for five seconds, we'd capture a different amount of water in our bucket. Although our aperture (plastic sheet) was the same size as last time, our shutter speed (the length of time we poured the water) was shorter, so there was less time for the bucket to capture as much water.

Using different combinations of apertures and shutter speeds enables cameras to capture different quantities of light. This is important because the aperture and the shutter speed influence the final result of our photos in different ways.

Aperture

The aperture affects the depth of field of the photo. This means how much of our image is in focus - its sharpness. Imagine you have two photos, both of a friend standing in front of the Eiffel Tower. In one photo, your friend is clearly in focus; their image is nice and sharp, but the Eiffel Tower, behind them, is all blurred. In the next photo, your friend is all nice and sharp, and so is the Eiffel Tower. It is the camera's aperture that has created these two effects.

Why is this important? It all depends upon what you want your photo to illustrate. If you were taking a photograph of a flower, you might want the stamen to look sharp, and for the flower's background to be blurred, because you want people to look at the flower, not the background.

THE DIGITAL WORLD 31

Focus is on the flower, so the background is blurred.

Whereas, if you were taking a photo of a fantastic view you might want as much of the scene to be in focus as possible.

Most of the foreground and background is in focus in this view of Tarn Hows in the Lake District.

So, the aperture affects how much of your photograph is in focus.

Shutter Speed

The shutter speed determines how movement is captured in your photo. Imagine you're taking a photograph of a waterfall. A slow shutter speed means that light is let into the camera for a longer time. Half a second might not seem long, but the water flowing over the waterfall will look blurred because it will have moved quite a long way during that half a second. The photo has captured more of the movement in the scene in front of you. Setting a faster shutter speed, such as a thousandth of a second, will appear to freeze time. The water flowing over the waterfall will not travel far in a thousandth of a second, so your photograph might look as though each droplet of water has been frozen in time.

A slow shutter speed captures the movement of water in a waterfall.

THE DIGITAL WORLD   33

A faster shutter speed will freeze the movement of water in a waterfall.

Therefore, the shutter speed determines how much movement you capture in your photo.

If you're taking a photograph of lots of moving things, a faster shutter speed will help to freeze the action. This may mean that more of the photograph is sharp and in focus. A longer shutter speed will capture the movement, so some elements in the photo, such as moving cars, or people, will be blurred.

Because many cameras offer different programme modes (landscape, portrait, action, etc) you don't need to worry too much about these two processes. (Professional photographers tend to want to set these individual elements themselves when capturing a photograph.) However, there will be times when it can be useful to understand what the camera is doing, so you can choose the right mode on your camera to capture the image you want.

Sensitivity

There is a third element that influences the amount of light captured by a digital camera: the sensitivity of the camera sensor. Professional photographers are interested in this, but, for this book, it's not something we need to be concerned with. (You may hear it being referred to as the ISO.)

Capturing a Photo

Digital cameras process a lot of information quickly. To take a photo, usually, you press a button. (On a mobile phone you might touch the screen.) However, the process of capturing the photo involves two stages. On a camera, pressing the button half-way will get it to focus on the scene in front of you. The camera's LCD screen may illustrate which part of your photo it is focusing on, such as people's faces. Whilst it is doing this, it is also assessing the amount of light and considering the scene in front of you to determine what sort of photo is being taken. This is where the camera is deciding what aperture and shutter speed it should use. When you press the button down completely, the camera uses this information to take the photo at that time. Milliseconds later, the computer wizardry built into your camera has processed all of this digital information and displays it on the LCD screen. (On a smartphone, there may be a short delay between you touching the screen and the phone taking the photo.)

Understanding (Mega) Pixels

All digital cameras capture a photographic image on a light sensor. This sensor converts the light into electronic data, which the camera's processor uses to create the photograph. These sensors comprise of millions of pixels. One pixel is a tiny element, or fragment, of a picture. (The word pixel comes from **PIC**ture **EL**ement.) A megapixel is a million pixels.

The more megapixels a camera's sensor has, the more detailed information it can capture. This might suggest that cameras with more megapixels can take better quality photos, however, it's not as simple as that. There is a difference between the 16-megapixel sensor in your mobile phone's camera and the 16-megapixel sensor in a mirrorless or compact camera.

I mentioned earlier how a camera uses the aperture and the shutter speed to determine how much light reaches the camera's sensor, and I gave the example of pouring water through a hole into a bucket. Think of the bucket as one pixel. So a 16-megapixel sensor is like having 16 million buckets all collecting light. It's the size of these buckets that affects picture quality. Bigger buckets mean more detail. They can hold more light (digital information). Therefore, while a 16-megapixel sensor in your mobile phone's camera has just as many pixels as the 16-megapixel sensor in your compact camera, the compact camera's sensor will have bigger pixels that are capable of capturing more light information. Likewise, a 16-megapixel sensor in a digital SLR camera will have bigger pixels than a 16-megapixel sensor in a compact camera.

Technology is advancing all of the time, which means that sensor quality is improving, too. However, from a writer's point of view, it's important to understand that the number of megapixels your camera has will determine how your photos might be used in a magazine. For that, we need to look at print resolution.

Print Resolution

In magazines and publications, everything we see is made up of lots of tiny dots. That includes the words, as well as the pictures. Years ago, if you looked closely enough at a photograph in a newspaper you could see those individual dots. Today's publishing processes print those dots so small the naked eye can't see them. And it's this that influences whether, and how, an editor can use our photos.

You may have come across the terms DPI (dots per inch) or PPI (pixels per inch). Technically, there is a difference between the two, but for the sake of this book, it's not a difference we need to concern ourselves with. Most publications print at a resolution of 300 pixels per inch, which is the resolution where the naked eye can't see those individual dots.

A camera's sensor is usually rectangular. My camera's sensor is 5,616 pixels wide by 3,744 pixels tall, and this means the total number of pixels it has is:

$$5{,}616 \times 3{,}744 = 21{,}026{,}304.$$

So my camera sensor has over 21 million pixels (or 21 megapixels).

If every inch of a published photograph contains 300 pixels, then the maximum size my photos can be used at is:

$$(5{,}616 \text{ pixels} \div 300 \text{ pixels per inch}) \times (3{,}744 \text{ pixels} \div 300 \text{ pixels per inch}) \text{ or } 18.72 \text{ inches} \times 12.48 \text{ inches}.$$

In the UK, many magazines are A4 in size, which means a double-page spread is an A3 size. An A3 sheet of paper is 16.53 inches wide by 11.69 inches tall. So you can see that my camera produces photos that can be published at 300dpi at a size that's slightly bigger than A3. That's more than ample for most magazines, but it does mean that if the editor wants to use one of my photos as a double-page spread they can do.

If a camera's sensor is 3,456 pixels wide by 2,304 pixels tall, then it has a total of 7,962,624 pixels. This would be classified as an 8-megapixel camera (What's a few pixels between friends?). Printing at 300ppi, this would produce a photograph of 11.52 inches by 7.68 inches, which is just under A4 size. These days, most cameras have at least twice this many megapixels, so they're capable of producing publishable photos that can be printed at a size of A4 or larger.

Why is this important? Because the size of your images influences *how* they are used in a publication. While my images are big enough to be used as a double-page spread, the editor doesn't have to use them at that size. They can shrink them down to any size they want. What they can't do, is take a small photo and make it bigger. When you 'blow up' a photo beyond 300 pixels per inch, the naked eye then begins to see each pixel, which renders the photo useless to an editor.

So, the more megapixels your camera has, the larger the photos it is capable of producing. This offers the editor more flexibility. Remember, the number of megapixels isn't the only deciding factor, the quality of the pixels is important too. But if you're buying a new compact camera, a 16-megapixel camera will produce bigger photos than a 10-megapixel camera.

It is possible, through the use of image processing software, to get bigger photos from smaller files. This technique is known as interpolation, where the software creates new pixels and then tries to guess what information should be in these new pixels, based upon the information contained in the surrounding pixels. It can work well when making photos slightly bigger, but it can't turn a 2-inch-square photo in an A3-sized image.

Image Quality Settings

Another way to ensure you offer the editor the best quality images your camera is capable of taking is to check out the image quality settings on your camera. (You might need to check your camera's manual, but you'll probably be able to find the option by browsing through your camera's settings.)

Some cameras offer the option to change the image quality of the photos it takes: High Quality (HQ), or Super High Quality (SHQ). Always set your camera to the highest quality available. Lower settings will produce smaller, lower quality images, which is not what you want. Manufacturers offer this choice because lower quality settings produce smaller file sizes, which use less space on your memory card. It's better to set your camera to the highest setting available and buy some spare memory cards!

If you've taken photos on your mobile phone and you want to share them with someone else, your phone may ask you to select an image quality setting (eg: small, medium, high, actual size). Always select the *actual size*. This will ensure your recipient gets the best quality image.

Digital File Types

When you write an article or story in your word processor and then save it, your computer gives it a file type extension. Microsoft Word files are saved as *docx* documents. These file-type extensions tell the computer which software programme to open to view the file with.

When your camera takes a photo and saves it to the memory card, most cameras save the photo with a file type called JPEG (.jpg), pronounced "jay-peg". This is the file type that most magazines and publishers use. Whenever I send any photos to editors, I send them in jpeg format.

Your camera's setting might offer you some other file types:

- TIFF - this is a better file type because the file stores more image information than is held in a jpeg image. This means that TIFF files are larger than JPEG files. While most publications will be able to use a TIFF file, they generally all ask for jpeg files. (Some photography magazines like TIFF files, but if you want to send photos to these markets you're moving on somewhat from the realms of this book.)
- RAW - this is like the digital equivalent to the film that photographers used to use before photography went digital. RAW files are best for professional and serious amateur photographers because these files retain much more light information. However, once the picture has been taken, the photographer has to transfer the data to a computer and then process the image in some software to produce a JPEG file. This is what is known as the digital darkroom because photographers are 'developing' the image to create the photo they want.
- RAW + JPEG - some cameras offer the option to save files in both the RAW and JPEG formats at the same time. It should be remembered that this option will use up more of your memory card because there will be two copies of every photo that you take. If your interest in digital photography grows, this is something to consider for the future.

Writers looking to offer editors some useful photos to accompany their words will find the JPEG format is sufficient.

3

TAKING PHOTOGRAPHS

With your camera set to save photos at the highest quality setting, and in jpeg format, it's now time to take some photos. There are many books that can tell you how to take better, or more creative, photographs, and I hope, in the future, you'll be inspired to look at some of them. However, here are a few basic points I believe every writer should consider as they compose their shots, which will make your photos more useful to an editor.

Understanding Programme Modes

Most cameras have an automatic mode. If your compact camera has a small dial on the top, it may appear as a green rectangle or the word AUTO in green. Cameras with touch-screen LCDs may simply have Automatic as one of the options.

The camera's automatic mode can be very good at capturing useful photos, and it is a great place to start. However, it can't always correctly assess the scene you're pointing your camera at, so it can make mistakes. Digital cameras can be fooled, resulting in blurred, dark or overly-bright images, which are of no use to anyone.

Sometimes it can be useful to select another of the camera's modes to capture the image you want. And remember, it doesn't cost you anything to take the same scene using different modes and comparing the results. Play about!

Head and Shoulders: This setting is for taking portraits of people who are standing still. In Chapter 2 we saw how the camera's aperture affects the depth of field: how much of the photo is in focus. This setting selects an aperture that will focus on the people but make the background look blurred. (Many cameras have face detection facility, so it will focus automatically at your subject's face.) So, if you want to take a photo of a group of people, but the setting they're in isn't important, this mode will capture an image that makes the background slightly blurred, thus drawing your eye to the people.

Remember: this is for shots of people standing still. The shutter speed will be relatively slow, so it's best used for when people pose to have their photo taken.

Mountains: This is ideal for scenic views. Here, the camera sets an aperture that will try to have as much of the photo in focus as possible. Most of the foreground and the background will be sharp and clear. This mode is perfect for natural views of mountains, rolling hills and wide-open spaces, as well as man-made views of cityscapes: when there isn't much moving around. If you want a photo of some people posing for the camera, but you want the background to be in focus too, select this mode rather than the portrait mode.

Flower: This is for close-ups: an insect on a flower, for example. This tells the camera to focus on something close to the end of its lens and then sets an aperture throwing the background out of focus, so the sharpest area is of the object in the foreground. Experiment with this mode. You might find it produces better results when you want to capture the smaller details of objects, such as the carvings on a stone, or in a piece of wood, or the mosses and lichens growing on a wall. It's not just for flowers.

Running Man: This mode selects a faster shutter speed, designed to freeze any movement and produce a sharper image. It's useful for any type of movement (not just running men). If you want to freeze the water in a waterfall, capture a racing car, planes flying overhead, or a passing train, then try this mode. If you're standing in the middle of a particularly bustling market with lots of people moving about, select this option. This mode isn't just for sporting activities, but for any movement. Some cameras have a children-and-pets setting, which does the same thing: it increases the shutter speed because children and pets are notorious for moving about. (It may also activate the face detection technology.)

Moon and Stars: Yes, this is for night-time shots, but it isn't just for taking photos after dark. This mode is also useful in other low-light settings, such as poorly-lit interiors, like churches, houses, cafes and restaurants. This mode may trigger the camera's flash unit to fire, spreading more light onto the subject.

Crossed Out Lightning Bolt: This turns off the camera's flash facility, if it has one, which most compact cameras and mobile phones do. It's something to consider when entering properties, such as tourist attractions, where flash photography is not permitted because objects in the room are sensitive to light. The camera will make the necessary adjustments to get enough light onto the sensor, which may include having a longer shutter speed. This means you will need to hold the camera still whilst it is taking the picture to avoid any blurring.

Turning off the flash is also useful if your background is reflective, such as a mirror, or a window. Some of the light from your flash will bounce off the reflected surface and affect your shot.

Other Modes: Some cameras offer a multitude of other modes, such as beach, winter or fireworks mode. These all take into consideration the amount of light available. In beach and winter scenes, cameras can be confused by how much light there is. A lot of light is reflected by the whiteness of snow, or the sand on a beach, making cameras think there's more light than there is. The resulting photos come out dark and subdued. These settings attempt to over-ride this.

Play About

The beauty of digital cameras is you can play about and experiment. If you don't like what you see on your LCD screen then delete the photo and try again. Consider taking two photos: take one using the auto mode and then take another using a different mode that you think might be appropriate. Compare the two images and keep whichever one you like most. Over time, you'll learn which mode works best for which situation.

Top Tip: *Always switch your camera back to Auto mode after taking a photo in another mode. That way, should a situation suddenly present itself you can press the button to take a picture and your chances of capturing something useable are greatly increased. If you'd recently taken a photo using the Mountain mode for a view and left this mode selected and then a fast-moving scene were to suddenly appear (such as an air-display of fast-flying jets) your camera would struggle to cope because it is set for a scene where nothing is moving. Having your camera on*

Auto mode would give it a fighting chance of capturing something.

Planning the Images You Need

Professional photographers use tripods, not only to hold the camera steady but also to slow them down. Setting up a tripod and attaching the camera to it takes time. Time, which the professional photographer uses to think about the shot they're going to take and how they're going to compose it.

The beauty of mobile phone cameras and compact cameras is that you can simply point them at the view you want to take and then press the button. With these cameras, it's possible to point, click; point, click; point, click. Although that has advantages, it also has drawbacks. Planning can improve your photographs dramatically.

- Survey the scene. Take a moment to look at what you want to photograph. How many times do you take a photo and then later spot the overflowing litter bin in the corner, or the builder's van jutting into the frame? Simply taking stock of what's in front of you and considering whether you want it in your picture is enough to make you think about how to frame it. You might move your camera to the right, slightly, to avoid the builder's van. Or you could til it up slightly to avoid the litter bin.
- Glance around the edges. When you look through your viewfinder, or at the camera's LCD screen, start at the bottom left-hand corner and look along the left-hand edge, then go along the top edge, down the right-hand edge and back along the bottom. It's a simple habit, but you'd be surprised how many times

you can avoid cutting off people's heads or feet when you do this. And it often identifies those other annoying things that creep into photos, such as street signs, lamp-posts or publicity A-boards.

- What will your readers want to see? If you're taking photos to illustrate an article or a book, then think about the point you're going to be explaining to your readers. Plan your shot around that. For example, if you're writing a travel article and want to tell people about the view from your hotel bedroom window, take a photo from the window, but consider taking a photo that includes the window frame. The window frame proves to the reader that the view is from the window.

Include the window frame if you want to show readers the view is what you can see though the window.

Likewise, if you want to illustrate that the hotel is a stone's throw from the beach, take a picture that includes the front of the hotel and the beach.

- Zoom in. If you're writing about an impressive statue in the town park, make sure that statue fills your LCD screen or viewfinder. Don't have it as a pinprick in the middle of your picture. That might help set the scene, but it doesn't show the reader how impressive it is.

This photo of the Wilfred Owen statue sets the scene, but doesn't show it in detail.

So, zoom in (walk closer if you have to) and make the subject of your photo fill the frame. If the statue has an intricately carved section, zoom in on that so the reader can see it for themselves.

> ***Top Tip:*** If your camera has Image Stabilisation (it might be abbreviated to IS) then switch it on. Whenever we hold a camera, even the smallest of hand movements can cause an image to blur. When you zoom in on a subject, any such movement is exaggerated further. The image stabiliser helps to counteract this.

Close up of Wilfred Owen statue.

Light

Photography is all about capturing light, and many books explore the intricacies of how light affects the images we capture. There are some basic points to consider, concerning light, when taking your photos.

- Where is your light source? Shooting directly into the sun can be dangerous, but is also more likely to confuse your camera's light meter, as it decides what aperture and shutter speed it needs. Better-lit photos tend to have the sun/light source to your side or behind you.

Avoid shooting directly into the sun (and NEVER look directly at the sun through a camera's viewfinder).

- Consider the time of day. Where in the sky the sun is will affect any shadows in your photo. Photographers love the first hour after sunrise and the hour before sunset, because the sun's light is softer. However, it's not always practical to take photos at this time of day. Look at the scene you are taking. How big are the shadows? Do they dominate your image? If so, try shooting from a different angle to reduce this. Avoid getting your own shadow in the photo. The light changes throughout the year, as the seasons change, so take the opportunity to capture photos of places you regularly go to, throughout the year.

Long shadows can be distracting. Avoid getting your own shadow in the photo.

Seek Out Unusual Angles

While you're planning your shots before you take them, consider changing your viewpoint. We tend to see the world from our most usual viewpoint: standing upright. Anything taken from a different position can be more intriguing. Might you get a more interesting photo of the statue if you were to sit on the ground and shoot upwards, rather than standing a short distance away and taking the photo straight on? If you want to capture the sea rolling onto the beach, instead of standing up and taking the photo, why not lie down on the beach and take it from ground level? (Take care not to get sand or seawater on your camera though.)

A statue of Charles Darwin outside Shrewsbury Library.

Viewing something from a different angle offers a new perspective on a scene. You don't have to take every photo from an unusual angle, but just remember to experiment from time to time.

A statue of Charles Darwin outside Shrewsbury Library, but from a different angle.

Photo Orientation - Landscape and Portrait

Get into the habit of taking two photos: one landscape, one portrait. Most cameras, when held against the eye so that the shutter button is to the right of the lens, take photos in landscape format. This means that the photo is wider than it is taller. A double-page spread in a magazine is landscape format.

A photo in landscape format: ideal for a double-page spread.

If you rotate the camera by 90 degrees, you're now shooting in portrait, and the photo will be taller than it is wider. Most magazine front covers are portrait shots. A single page photo in a magazine is usually portrait.

Taking photos in both formats offers the editor flexibility. When climbing on The Wrekin, in Shropshire, I took two photos of The Needle's Eye, a rock formation on the side of the hill with extensive views behind it: one was landscape, the other portrait. One magazine editor used the landscape version for a double-page spread, and the portrait version was used as the front cover.

The same image, but taken in portrait aspect: ideal for front covers.

If you can provide both formats it gives the editor choice. Our view of the world is in landscape format and so it is what we're used to seeing (which is why our televisions have all gone widescreen). Rotating your camera 90 degrees alters the way we see a view and it might offer a more visually pleasing image than the landscape format. It's all about experimenting.

Understanding the Rule of Thirds

Just like writing has its rules, such as: avoid using clichés (like the plague), so, too, does photography. (And just like writing rules, photography rules can be broken too.) One useful guideline for image composition is the Rule of Thirds.

Take a sheet of paper and place it on a table in front of you. With a ruler, draw two straight lines from top to bottom, so that you create three equal-width columns across the page. Do the same again, but this time from left to right, to create three equal-sized rows. This creates nine separate sections, and four intersections, where the two vertical lines bisect the two horizontal lines.

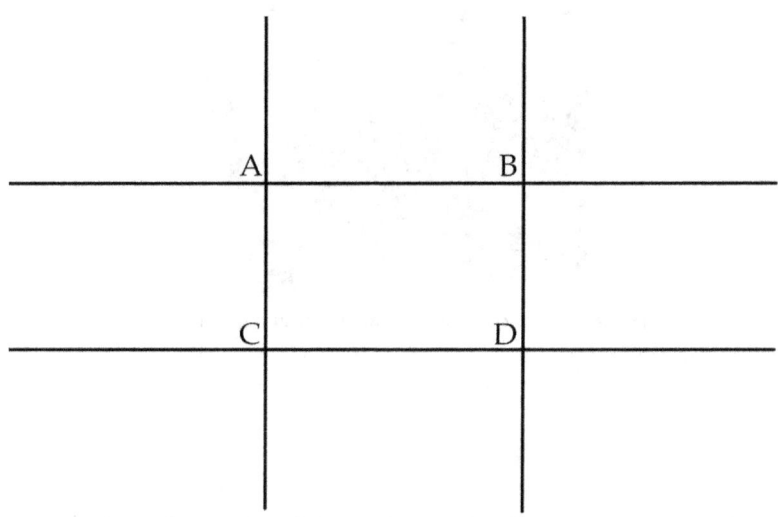

Imagine two horizontal lines and two vertical lines sub-dividing your image into nine equal-sized areas.

When viewing a photograph, our eyes tend to fall more naturally on these points where the lines bisect each other (points A, B, C or D), rather than the centre of the photograph. Some cameras have the facility to display similar lines in their viewfinders or on their LCD screens to help with image composition.

Placing the subject of your photograph at one of these four points (A, B, C or D) may make the composition more pleasing to the eye, rather than sticking it right in the middle square of the photograph.

In the photo overleaf, you'll see that I've placed the tall rocky outcrop (called the Lone Shepherd) along the left-hand vertical line (joining points A to C), rather than in the middle of the photo. This is a more pleasing composition (to me!) and also allows the summit of Sugar Loaf hill to sit near the centre of the image. Had I placed the Lone Shepherd in the middle of the frame, the summit of Sugar Loaf would have been closer to the right hand edge of the frame. Using the *Rule of Thirds* has improved this image in this instance.

The Lone Shepherd, lined up along the left-hand vertical line when using the Rule of Thirds composition.

We can also use the horizontal lines to help with composition. Imagine, for example, you were taking a photograph of a beach scene, and the horizon (where the sea meets the sky) is in the middle of the photograph. Some people feel that because the horizon creates a line across the middle of the photo it cuts the image in half. If nothing interesting is happening in the sky, all of the action, or interest, is taking place in the bottom half of the photo, which wastes the top half of the image.

The horizon practically cuts this image in half …
although the flag sits neatly on the left-hand
vertical line of the Rule of Thirds composition.

If you place the horizon nearer to the top of the photo, such as along the rule of thirds line that separates the top row from the middle row (A to B in our image earlier), it offers a slightly different perspective. This will mean there's less sky, but more beach.

In this photo, the horizon sits higher up the frame, and we see more beach but less sky.

Alternatively, you could tilt your camera up, slightly, which would place the horizon along the lower of the two horizontal lines, separating the middle row from the bottom row (line C to D). This means your photo now has twice as much sky as beach, but it may look more satisfying than an image that is half sky and half beach.

This photo has the horizon set low, so we see more sky and less beach.

Whilst it's called the Rule of Thirds, it is only a *guideline*. There are many photographers out there who detest the Rule of Thirds and avoid using it when composing their images. That's fine. Creativity is all about how we want to interpret something. What I'm suggesting here is that you experiment. Try it and see what you think. Moving your subject matter to a different place on your screen might help you create a photograph that is far more pleasing to the eye.

4

PHOTOGRAPHY LEGALITIES

Photographers should exercise caution at all times because there are restrictions as to what you can photograph. Rules vary from country to country, so always research any regulations that may apply to your destination. Check out the rules relating to your own country of residence too. Please remember that regulations and laws can change, so what I discuss here was relevant at the time of writing, but could change in the future. As the photographer, it is always your responsibility to check what laws and regulations apply. Here, though, are some general points to consider.

Do You Need Permission?

So many people have cameras these days, it's easy to assume we can take photos where we like. Some places have no objections to people taking photos for private, personal, use. However, if you're taking photos that will be published, permission may be required in some situations:

- In a public place. In many countries, people are permitted to take photos if they are in a public place, such as on a street or footpath. (That's why the paparazzi can do what they do here in the UK, snapping photos of celebrities out shopping.) This also means that, generally, you can take photos of private buildings, as long as you're standing in a public place. Of course, you should exercise caution. Some military and national security establishments may ban the taking of photos within a certain area, on the grounds of national security.

- On private property. Once you step onto private property, you *may* need to obtain permission. The property owner can ask people not to take photos, but just because you're on private property that doesn't mean that you can't take photos. The simple solution is to ask for permission upon arrival. Confusingly, some places you might perceive to be public areas are actually private. Shopping centres may be bustling with people, but many are private property. So if someone asks you to stop taking photos you should abide by that request. Some properties, like churches and cathedrals, ask photographers to buy a permit, for a small fee.
- Taking photos of people. Generally (although laws around the world vary), if you're in a public place, photographing people is permitted. If you were taking a photo of a busy market place, with stalls set up along the public road, then you don't need permission from the people who happen to be shopping at those stalls. (The practicalities of getting permission would be a nightmare.) However, privacy laws vary across the world, with some countries being more restrictive than others, so again, when travelling abroad do some research. In the vast majority of cases, common sense will tell you what is and isn't acceptable. Taking a photo of a beach packed with

people should be acceptable, but standing on a public street with a huge zoom lens to take a photo through the window of someone sitting in their private home would be seen as an invasion of privacy. Likewise, exercise care when children are about. Taking a wide shot of a public place that includes lots of people, some of whom happen to be children, shouldn't cause any problems. Remember that in some countries taking someone's photo might be culturally offensive.

Commercial Photography versus Editorial Photography

There are places (such as London's Trafalgar Square) where commercial photography is managed and fees need to be paid to take photographs at these locations. Commercial photography typically includes photos taken for advertisements, brochures, greetings cards, posters, corporate events and merchandise that will be sold to the public.

When a photograph is used to illustrate an article or a book it is known as *editorial* use, which is not the same as *commercial* photography. Therefore, commercial photography restrictions shouldn't apply to writer/photographers. However, when someone is seen taking photographs in a managed area, it's not possible to determine whether they're taking photos for personal, editorial or commercial use, which is why security guards and officials may approach you to check. If you're travelling to a specific destination to take photos, always check before travelling whether any restrictions apply. You may need a permit to take photos for editorial use, so it's worth applying for these in advance.

Remember, too, that if you're granted permission to take photographs for editorial use in an area where commercial photography is restricted, you can only use those photos for editorial purposes. Using them in the future for commercial opportunities will break regulations.

Essentially, if you exercise common sense, you shouldn't experience too many difficulties. Consider whose property you're on to determine whether you need to ask permission, and if travelling some distance to visit a particular destination you would be wise to research before travelling whether any photographic restrictions apply. When photographing other people, think about how you might feel if someone were taking a photo of you. Asking for someone's permission, even though you might not legally need it, is simply polite and courteous.

We often assume that if we were to walk up to a stranger and ask their permission they will refuse. In reality, they often respond positively. An interesting exercise some photography courses encourage students to undertake is to approach strangers and ask for permission to take their photo. The task requires them to get twenty strangers to agree and another twenty strangers to refuse. Most students find it takes far longer to find people who refuse permission.

Release Forms

Release forms are generally used for commercial photography, rather than editorial photography. Most writers don't need them. However, there may be some occasions when a release form is required for magazine purposes (such as photos of children) so it's worth having a little knowledge about them. Release forms fall into two categories: model and property. Model release forms are signed by the people who appear in a photograph, and property release forms are signed by the property owner or a member of staff employed at the property.

For editorial purposes, particularly in the UK, release forms are, generally, not required. The problem arises in some countries where the definition of commercial photography varies. In these areas, a publication might ask if the photographer has signed release forms for those photographs. If you don't have signed release forms, it means the publication won't use those images.

A model or property release form is a document that proves the people, or the property owner, have given permission for the photograph to be used for commercial purposes. For most writers, this isn't a problem, because in the majority of cases their photos are being used for editorial purposes.

Remember: you don't need a release form to *take* the photo. However, not having a release form will prevent you from selling the photo for commercial use in the future. It will restrict where you can offer that photograph for sale.

For example, if you take a head-and-shoulders photo of an African tribesman, you might feel this photo encapsulates the essence of the people you met on your travels, so it would make a great illustration for your travel article. For most magazines and publishers a model release isn't necessary because the photo is being used for editorial purposes. However, if a company approached you and said they wanted to use that image on a T-Shirt, calendar, or poster, to advertise their product, this would be commercial use, for which a model release form would be required.

An occasion where editors may ask to see model release forms is if you're taking photos of individual children (aged under 18) to illustrate your article. Editors will want to see signed permission from the child's parent or guardian, confirming they're happy for those photographs to be used in this way.

Copyright

Copyright exists as soon as you create something. When a writer puts words on a page they own the copyright in those words, and that copyright exists for their entire lifetime, continuing until the end of the 70th year after their death. Copyright enables writers to licence their work (and charge for it, thus benefitting from their creativity).

Copyright exists for all creative artists, including painters, musicians, sculptors and photographers. This means you own the copyright in every photograph you take (even if it isn't taken on your camera). You're the creator, not the camera.

Some writers think that material on the Internet is copyright-free and available for anyone to use. That is not true. All material is subject to copyright, no matter where it appears. Therefore, you can't help yourself to a photograph from the Internet and use it to illustrate your article, because you don't own the copyright. Using such images, without permission, is theft. How would you like it if someone helped themselves to your words, without asking? (There's a practical reason for not doing this, too. Remember print resolution? Most images on the Internet are displayed at 72 or 96 pixels per inch, which makes them pretty unusable in a print publication requiring 300 pixels per inch.)

There are some websites where high-resolution photos are made available for editorial use, and we'll look at these in Chapter 6. The difference with these images is that creators have granted permission for them to be used editorially, subject to being properly credited. They will also be of a high enough quality for print reproduction.

Don't forget, it's the photographer who usually owns the copyright in the photograph, not the owner of the photograph. If you're writing an article about someone and they give you a photo of themselves for possible illustration purposes, even though they might own the photo, you'll need to check with the person who took the photograph (who might still own the copyright) whether you can use it.

How many times have you stopped a stranger at a popular tourist site and asked them to take a photo of you and a friend/partner on your camera? Even though the photo is of you, and it was taken on your camera, the copyright lies with the stranger you stopped to take the photo. They were the visual creator. They determined the composition. *They* own the copyright.

If you take your own photos then you own the copyright, which makes life so much easier.

It's copyright that allows us to exploit opportunities to license the use of our images. For someone else to use our work they have to get our permission. The best way to do this is for us to issue them with a license, and we can charge for this (if we want). In reality, when it comes to magazines and publishers, it's rarely the photographer who names the price but the magazine that states what they're willing to pay. The point is, though, that as the copyright holder of the image we are in control of who uses it, in which medium and territory, and for how long.

Once you relinquish copyright, you no longer have the right to issue licenses to use the image and to charge for that license.

Photographic Rights Offered

Writers are used to offering publications specific rights in the words, such as First British Serialisation Rights, or First North American Serialisation Rights, or more commonly these days, all rights. But what about the photographic rights in an illustrated article?

Generally, magazines buy a licence to use the image once, alongside the words they are buying. You might see this referred to as *One-Time Reproduction Rights*. If the publication wanted to use your photographs again, they'd have to get in touch and pay for one-time reproduction rights again.

However, many magazines now have digital versions (for viewing on tablets and computers) and websites, so they require more than one-time reproduction print rights. They might ask for electronic rights, for a limited period, such as for the duration of the issue your words and pictures will appear. Alternatively, they may ask for a non-exclusive right to use your photos electronically for a longer period.

You should exercise caution if the publication asks for a licence that limits your rights in any way, or they ask for exclusivity. Limited exclusivity might be appropriate; it depends on how long the exclusivity is for. However, if the publication asks for all rights, they're effectively asking for copyright. If you sell all of the rights to your photos, you have no rights left to exploit. Ever.

When it comes to our words, we can always rewrite them. If I write a travel piece about a particular destination and the publication buys *All rights* in those words, it means I can't resell the same article (those words in that order) anywhere else. But that doesn't stop me from writing a brand new piece about the same travel destination.

But you can't do that with a photograph. Once you've sold all rights in that photograph there is nothing else you can do with that photograph.

Now, if the photograph is of somewhere local, it might be relatively easy to go and take another one. But you won't get a duplicate image, because there are so many variables. The weather may be different (if you're in the UK then it WILL be different!). The lighting in your photograph will be affected by the time of day. Shadows are harsher during the middle of the day than at the start or end of the day. Something physical might have changed. A different season will mean that foliage will be different.

So if you do sell all rights in a photograph, think about what it will take to enable you to go and take a new photograph of the same subject. Photographs from a once-in-a-lifetime holiday are, by their definition, irreplaceable.

Things can change on the ground, too.

In 2019, English Heritage spent millions of pounds refurbishing the world's first iron bridge, at Ironbridge, near Telford. For years, the bridge had been painted in a battleship-grey colour. But during the refurbishment, they found evidence of the bridge's original colour: rusty-red. So it was refurbished in that rusty-red colour.

You can't take a photo of a battleship-grey iron bridge at Ironbridge now. It doesn't exist!

Always negotiate if a magazine asks for more rights than you want to offer. In most situations, I've been able to negotiate something that suits both parties. One publication asked for all rights in my images. I said that wasn't possible because I'd already sold the rights in some of the images to a calendar company. The magazine accepted this and told me to write on my invoice the rights I was offering. I granted them one-time reproduction rights.

Another magazine asked for all rights in any of my photos accompany my words. I explained that this wasn't possible because I sell my photos through various outlets, and the photos I offer with my words are frequently taken from my photographic library (of over 15,000 images). In the end, we negotiated a contract that took one-time reproduction rights in any images I offered from my stock of photos, but if the editor sent me somewhere on a commission to take photos, then the magazine would have a six-month exclusivity arrangement on those commissioned photographs after publication. Once that six-month exclusivity period has expired I am free to do what I like with those images.

If ever you're unsure which rights a magazine or publisher wants in your photos, make sure you find out. Ask the editor, and get it in writing.

Watermarking

You may come across photographs that have the copyright symbol © followed by the photographer's name overlaid across an image. It's usually semi-opaque. You can still see the image through the text, but it's opaque enough to see the photograph's name and the copyright symbol.

Photographers do this, particularly when sharing an image online, such as on their website or social media channels. That way, should anyone else share the image it's quite clear who the copyright belongs to, and it cuts down the illegal use of images without the photographer's permission.

It's possible to place such watermarks on your images using the software I mention in the next chapter. Whatever you do, only use the watermarks when sharing your images online in some way. When sending them to a magazine to accompany your words, always send them copies of the images without the watermark showing.

PHOTOGRAPHY LEGALITIES 69

A photo with my watermark in the bottom right corner.

5

YOUR PERSONAL DIGITAL PHOTOGRAPHIC LIBRARY

It doesn't take a lot of snapping to create a decent-sized photographic library, so it's worth thinking about how you're going to organise them. The beauty of taking photos is that while you might be taking them for one particular project, such as an article, or a book, once you have them you can use them to illustrate other pieces of your work too. I have used/sold some of my photos several times over to illustrate different articles. Sometimes, that image taken ten years ago is just what you need to illustrate today's article.

What you need then is a system that allows you to find the right images when you need them.

Creating a Manageable Filing System

There's no definitive filing system, so you should create a filing system that works best for you. It doesn't matter how easy or complicated it is, all that's important is that you can find the images you want when you need them.

Most computer systems have a folder called *My Photos* or *My Pictures*. This can be a great place to start, but you can store your photos anywhere. I store mine in a folder called *Photographic Library* in *My Documents*. I do this because I make a regular backup of everything in the *My Documents* folder, so should the worst happen to my computer, I have back-up copies of both my words and my photos. Maintaining a folder called *Photographic Library* keeps my business images separate from my family photos (which tend to get filed in My Photos).

So, first of all, think about where you're going to store all of your photos.

Subject Matter Sorting: Once you've done that, think about the filing system that is right for you. How and where you file your photos might depend upon the sort of writing that you do. A travel writer, for example, might decide to have folders for each country they visit. It may then be sensible to create subfolders for each destination within that country.

A nature writer may decide to have folders for *Plants* and *Animals* and then have subfolders for each species and subspecies, whereas a gardening writer might prefer to have separate folders for *Hardy Plants, Half-Hardy Plants, Biennials* and *Perennials*, and then subfolders that group such plants into flower colour, or by Latin name.

Date Sorting: I use a date method. In my *Photographic Library* folder, I have a folder for each calendar year. Then, for each project, I save the day's photos in a folder that I name with the specific date and a brief description of the place or project. For example, on 13th March 2020, I explored Shrewsbury, in Shropshire, for a travel piece I was writing for a magazine. So, the file path for those images is as follows:

Photographic Library/2020/20200313 - Shrewsbury

So the day's photos are in a folder called *20200313 - Shrewsbury*, and this resides in my *2020* folder, which is in my

Photographic Library folder. I use the long date format of the year, month, date because this keeps everything in a strict date order, which I prefer. (Saving the date backwards makes sorting easier. If I saved the date in day/month/year format some computers might file 23022020 (23rd Feb) after 02032020 (2nd March) because, numerically, 23 comes after 02.)

- 20200313 - Shrewsbury
- 20200320 - Oswestry
- 20200412 - Fritilaries
- 20200420 - Helmeth Wood Bluebells
- 20200425 - Ragleth Hill
- 20200515 - Ludlow and Bromfield
- 20200519 - Caer Caradoc

My folder structure.

If I visited two different places on the same day, I create a different folder for each venue. They will have the same date format, but the location name afterwards will be different.

This system works well for me, but it might not be suitable for everyone. At the moment, my memory is fairly good, so I can remember which year I visited a place, which means I can go straight to the relevant year folder relatively quickly. However, I also use cataloguing software, which allows me to search my whole image library for specific photos with only a few key words.

Cataloguing Software

There is a choice of software programmes that can help you catalogue and organise your photographic library. Most of these will also allow you to process your images in some way (such as cropping, straightening, changing the exposure, etc).

Where this software comes in handy is that it enables you to add extra information to your photos, which makes it easier to find them amongst the many thousands of images you may accumulate over time.

It's possible that you already have one of these programmes installed on your computer. Examples include:

- Adobe Photoshop Elements
- Adobe Photoshop Lightroom
- Photos (Apple)
- OnOne Photo RAW
- Capture One

Not only do they allow you to add extra information to each photo, which then becomes searchable data, some also allow you to tag faces, or plot your photos on a map, which is useful if you need to see all the photos taken over the years of one particular person or every photo you've ever taken in a particular place.

Cataloguing software also allows you to flag, or rate your photos. For example, we can rate each photo out of 5 stars, and decide that we'll only offer editors photos that we've rated as 4 or 5-star. Searching by star-rating will bring up the relevant photos.

Another benefit of cataloguing software is that we can group our photos in a way that doesn't destroy our original folder structure. My folder structure saves all my photos by date. Therefore, the photos I took in the Lake District in 2009 are in a different folder to the Lake District photos I took in 2015 and 2019. However, I also tag each photo of the Lake District with a *Lake District* tag. Instead of having to find all of my folders that have photos from the Lake District on them, I simply click on my Lake District tag, and the software shows me all of the images I've tagged in this way.

Understanding Metadata and Keywording

Every time we take a photo with our digital camera, information is automatically recorded alongside it. This information is known as metadata. Our camera records information relating to the capture of the photograph, such as the shutter speed and aperture used, and whether the flash went off. Editors don't need to know this information (unless you're sending photos to a photographic magazine), so as a writer, this information isn't necessarily important to us.

However, most cataloguing software programmes will allow you to add extra information to the photo's metadata file, and this can be immensely useful. To find out how to add extra metadata to your photos, search the Help section of your cataloguing software.

You should consider adding the following metadata to every photo:

- A copyright notice: e.g. © your name.
- Contact details: a website, an email address, or a telephone number.

Any metadata that is added to the photo is saved to that particular image. Therefore, whenever you send a photo to an editor, they will be able to look at the metadata. By having your contact details and copyright associated with the photo, it reduces the risk of the photo being used without your permission. (Unscrupulous people will always find ways and means of getting around this, but if a reputable publisher or publication doesn't know to whom a photo belongs, one of the first places they look is in the photo's metadata.)

The cataloguing software also allows for the adding of a title or a description to each photo, which can then be saved as part of its metadata. I recommend doing this for every photo you take. It may seem a bit laborious (I often copy and paste a lot of the information for similar photos), but doing so is always time well spent.

I give each photo a title that includes a description of whatever is in the photo, along with details of where the photo was taken. This might include a road name, town, county, and regional description, as well as country. For example:

The Steam Yacht Gondola sailing across Coniston Water, near Coniston, the Lake District, Cumbria, England.

This is useful for two reasons:

- If an editor has lost your captions, they'll look at the metadata for a description.
- The cataloguing software will also search this description field when you enter a search term. If I search my photographic library for the word *Coniston*, then the earlier mentioned photo will appear in the results.

The Steam Yacht Gondola sailing across Coniston Water, near Coniston, the Lake District, Cumbria, England.

The more information you put into your metadata, the more searchable your photographic library becomes. Good cataloguing software can search this data in a fraction of a second. My photographic library has nearly 15,000 images and when I search for a specific term, all those images are scanned and the results offered to me within a second or so. That saves a lot of time in the long run.

Keywording

It's possible to take metadata one step further by allocating keywords. Keywords are words that you think might be useful to add to the photo's metadata, in addition to the information you add in the photo's title or caption. I mentioned earlier that cataloguing software often enables you to identify photos with certain people's faces in them so that you can bring up all of the photos a particular person appears in. Effectively, this face tagging is a form of keywording. Every time you tell the software that a photo has a particular person's face in it, the software adds their name to the keyword data of that photo.

How much keywording you do, if any, will depend upon the type of photos you take. Some photographers will add portrait or landscape as keywords to each photo, depending upon which way up the photo was taken. That way, if they only want to search for portrait shots, they'll search for this keyword. Other photographers might use moods, or emotions, as keywords. For example, a photograph of a ripple-free pond might have the following keywords added: *calm, tranquil, still*.

Keywording is one of those tools that develops as your library develops. A database is only as good as the information you can get out of it, and as your photographic library grows you'll begin to learn which keywords and phrases are most useful to you.

Adding Metadata Automatically

Many cataloguing software programmes allow us to add certain metadata automatically, so check whether your software has this facility. Most photographic software requires you to import your images into a catalogue. (You can choose to either import the image files or simply point the software to where your images are already saved on your computer.) It's during this import process that the software can automatically save some extra metadata to the photo as it imports the image. If you can, set it up so that every time you import photos, they are catalogued with your copyright and contact data.

Basic Image Processing

I mentioned earlier that these software programmes also allow us to undertake some basic processing of images to improve them. When I say *improve* I mean there are a few steps we can take to make our images more publishable, if something didn't go quite right when we took the photo. Some of these programmes are immensely sophisticated and are capable of doing amazing things to our images, if we have the time and the patience to learn how to use the software properly.

I recently switched from using Adobe Lightroom to Capture One and found the best way for me to learn was to watch video tutorials. If you can't work out how to do something with the software, search YouTube for a tutorial. Many software developers now put video tutorials up on their websites.

There may even be some Facebook groups set up for users of the software. I've joined a couple for Capture One, and not only do they post information about new video tutorials being added to the company's website, but there are also many experienced users on there who are happy to answer questions from newbies. (Sometimes I've found their help to be quicker than the official technical support.)

In Chapter 2, I mentioned how professional photographers take their images in RAW format and use computer software to process or develop those images. Most of the software programmes identified earlier will enable you to do this, so if you become more interested in photography, these software packages will grow with you.

For this book, there are a couple of quick fixes I want to mention that may help improve your photos and make them of more interest to an editor. Most of these software packages have a Quick Fix option which deals with the following:

Red-Eye Removal: When taking photographs in a dark environment the flash unit on your camera is likely to fire. A side effect of this is that people's eyes may appear to be devilishly red. This happens because our retinas reflect the red rays (found within white light) out of our eyes. When it's dark our pupils expand to draw in as much light as possible to help us see, which means when a flash goes off more of the red light is reflected back through them.

Some cameras have a Red-Eye Reduction option. This causes the flash on your camera to fire twice. The first flash happens a split second before you take the photo. The pupils in people's eyes contract quickly, because of the sudden bright light, so that when the second flash happens and the photo is taken our subject's pupils are much smaller and so less red light is reflected off the back of people's retinas. This can work quite well, but it isn't always perfect.

The software packages are quite good at resolving this. Generally, all you have to do is select the Red-Eye Removal option and then place your mouse pointer on the red eye and click. In most cases, this turns the pupils black. It isn't perfect all of the time, but it works most of the time. Always remove as much of the red-eye from your photos as you can. Editors don't like people with spooky eyes in photos.

Straightening and Cropping: It's not always easy to get your horizons straight. This often happens because we're too busy looking at the subject of our photo and so we forget to check the horizon behind it. Magazines are capable of resolving this but don't give them extra work to do. Do it yourself, and offer the magazine a better- looking image in the first place.

Of course, getting the horizon level or ensuring that Nelson's Column is not leaning precariously is best done before you press the shutter button. This is because the more you have to rotate your image to get things level, the more of your photo you will lose because it is cropped to retain its rectangular shape.

Always straighten out wonky horizons.

This is why it's useful to look at the photo on your camera's LCD screen when you've taken it. If you've got a really wonky photo, you're better off deleting it and taking another one.

As well as straightening, the software will also allow you to crop images. This allows you to cut some of your image from the top, bottom, left or right. It's particularly useful if someone has just started to walk into your photo as you've pressed the shutter button and you have someone's leg and arm entering your shot.

Sometimes, cropping the image can improve the composition. Again, be careful of cropping too much, because it makes your photo smaller, which may reduce its usability to an editor.

Cloning

Cloning is an option where we can remove something in our photo. This is achieved by copying a section from somewhere else in the photo and pasting it over the top. Think of it as *copy and paste* for pictures. I might use this if I spot that my not-quite-perfect sandy beach has a fizzy drink can littering it. Cloning allows me to copy a clean piece of the beach from elsewhere and paste it over the top of the fizzy drinks can. It can be useful sometimes to clone birds out of the sky, especially if they're flying fast and look a little blurred.

Notice how I've mentioned about using the cloning tool to alter minor points in the image. I believe a photo should offer a fair representation of what you are taking. Many of my articles are travel features, so the photos are there to show readers what a place looks like and, hopefully, inspire them to visit it too. Cloning out a particularly horrible-looking block of flats from a scene would give readers a false impression of the place. I did notice a magazine cloned out a couple of lamp-posts from one of my photos - but that was their decision.

Image Manipulation

It is amazing what these photo processing programmes are capable of. Some people have the skills to take out an overcast sky and replace it with a bright blue sunny one. I don't do that. I'm a writer who happens to do a bit of photo processing; I'm not a graphic designer.

If you find yourself getting interested in what the computer software is capable of, just be careful you don't get carried away. It's sometimes possible to identify these drastic image changes. For example, replacing an overcast sky with a clear blue, cloudless sky has its consequences. An overcast sky tends not to produce harsh shadows, whereas a clear blue sky means shadows should be more obvious. Once you've put the blue sky in, you then need to decide whereabouts in the sky the sun is, because even if you're not going to put a yellow orb in your photo, you still need to decide where your shadows are going to be, how big or small and at which angle they'll be falling on the ground. Play about with image manipulation too much and life starts getting complicated.

Having said that, computer software is making some sophisticated actions extremely simple now. One example I've seen is where the photographer can add the sun behind a stand of trees, and the software will work out where the rays filtering between the tree trunks should appear, depending upon where in the sky the sun is positioned.

Backing Up Your Photos

As your photographic library expands, and you spend more time adding metadata and descriptions to your images, backing up becomes imperative. If your hard drive blows up and you don't have a back-up copy, getting replicas of those 400 photos you took whilst on a once-in-a-lifetime safari holiday three years ago isn't going to be possible. Backing up needs to be a habit.

Firstly, invest in a back-up hard drive that uses back-up software to copy everything on your computer's hard drive. Both the latest versions of the Windows and Apple operating systems have a built-in back-up service that does all this automatically for you. Simply plug in a back-up hard drive, tell your computer to back up to it and it'll do the rest, usually on an hourly basis. For this back-up system, the capacity of the hard drive you plug in should be big enough to cope with all of your data (so use a hard drive with a storage capacity that is at least the same size as the hard drive in your computer, if not bigger).

I also do another back-up of my entire Photographic Library folder once a week. This goes onto a smaller, more portable backup drive, which I take with me when I go away (in case the house burns down while I'm not there).

You can buy online back-up storage space, which is useful because it protects you against any horrendous events, such as flooding, or fire, which might see your computer and the backups destroyed at the same time. Online (but off-site) back-up is useful, although online storage space becomes more expensive the more you need to back up. (And when you have a photographic library of over 15,000 images, that a lot of storage space.)

I also use Google Photos. (Yes, I use it as yet another backup.) At the time of writing, Google Photos gives users free, unlimited storage for photos of up to 16 megapixels. (I use my photographic software to create smaller, 16-megapixel copies of every image, which are then uploaded to my Google Photos account.) A 16-megapixel image will produce a photo of about 16 inches by 11 inches at 300 dots-per-inch, which isn't far off A4-size. So if a series of disasters were to happen that wiped out all of my backups, I would still have something on Google Photos. Those images wouldn't be big enough for an A3 double-page spread, but they'd be more than ample for most other magazine purposes.

Essentially, though, you can never have too many back-ups of your data (and that includes your words, as well as your photos).

Top Tip: When you import your photos onto your computer from your camera's memory card, do *NOT* delete the images from your camera's memory card just yet. If anything were to happen *to these images before your back-up systems have had a chance to do their work, you still have the originals on your camera's memory card. Some writers have two memory cards and swap them over each time, which means they have their most recently taken images hanging around for a little while longer.*

6
MAGAZINES

The biggest market for writers who can supply photos alongside their work is the magazine market. Publications are crying out for suitable images to accompany their articles, so it's worth spending time looking for the opportunities that exist.

Letters & Fillers

The great thing about these pages is that the magazines are not looking for images taken by professional photographers. They want snaps that any reader might have taken, including those taken on your mobile phone.

Magazines like readers' letter pages, because they offer an opportunity for interactivity between the publication and its readership. In some ways, readers' letter pages were the forerunners of today's social media, and just like Facebook, Instagram and Twitter, they love photos. Even better, some magazines pay more for letters with photos. So, what should you be looking out for?

Letters

- Read all of the letters on the page. What sort of topics are they discussing? How long are the letters: are they short, 50-word snippets or longer 200-word anecdotes?
- Make a note of whether every letter is accompanied by a photo. If *every* letter has a photo, then you *have* to supply a photo with any letter you might send to the page.
- Does the photograph illustrate the letter, or does the letter explain the photograph? It's a subtle difference, but an important one. On some letters pages, the photograph might be the main point of the page, and the letter explains what's going on in the photo. For example, a photo of a group of friends dressed up in fancy costumes might be accompanied by a couple of sentences explaining why these friends were dressed up like this, raising money for charity, perhaps.

Fillers

Some magazines also have filler pages. These are pages devoted to a collection of thoughts or snippets of information on a particular theme. One such example would be a page of household tips in a woman's magazine, which are often accompanied by photos. Another I see in some of the walking magazines are pages devoted to readers' photos taken while out doing the walking routes that have appeared in previous issues of the magazine. Study the images you see, so if you decide to target such a page, you can offer similar photos.

- Look at the size of the photos. Mobile phone images will be more than suitable.
- Don't take this the wrong way, but sometimes these

are quite boring images. However, they're published because they illustrate the point brilliantly. One writer sent in a tip explaining how she turned an empty fizzy drinks bottle into a cheap bird feeder. The accompanying photograph is of the bottle, half full of birdseed, hanging from a branch. It's not the most stunning and artistically creative photograph I've ever seen, but it's perfect for showing readers the household tip in action.

A squirrel inside a squirrel-proof bird feeder. An ideal photo for a Reader's Letter page.

- Think about how a photograph might improve your chances of publication. Stage the scene, if necessary. Spending two minutes to dress your props and set the scene could be two minutes that generate some useful money. Another reader explained how she used an old CD-rack as a spice rack. For the photo, she simply took an empty CD-rack, placed her spice jars in it, and put it in the kitchen. The photo clearly shows the different spice jars in the CD-rack, which is located near the cooker. Whether the spice rack stayed in situ, we'll never know, but this staging worked. So, if you have a tip, think about how you would illustrate it. (One reader mentioned how putting a horse chestnut tree conker in each corner of the room helped keep spiders away. She sold the tip by taking a photograph of a conker on the floor against the corner of the room's skirting boards.)
- Children and pets do the funniest things ... so

capture them with your camera. Many magazines have filler pages dedicated to these funny photos and pay well.

Magazines devoted to particular subjects or hobbies (gardening, sports, walking, photography, cars, or even travel), often have filler pages devoted to reader photographs. One travel magazine has a filler slot called Reader Postcards. Here, a reader submits one image from their latest travels, with about 75 words explaining where the photo was taken and why. A cookery magazine asks for readers' recipes and includes a photo of the finished dish. A photography magazine has a section dedicated to giving other photographers ideas about where to go to capture stunning scenery. Each place is accompanied by one photo, along with basic details on how to get there, and the best time of day to take photos.

All of these are opportunities a writer might dismiss, yet the writer/photographer can target them. Some pay money, whilst others offer prizes, but what they also do is offer an opportunity for you to get your name in front of the editor. One writer sent a letter into a magazine's letter page, accompanied by a photo, explaining the joys of a particular holiday destination. The editor got in touch and said the destination sounded wonderful, loved the photo, and asked if the writer had any more images and could write about the destination as a travel article instead. Naturally, the writer agreed and set to work. But this opportunity wouldn't have arisen had they not thought about sending a photo and a letter into the readers' letter page in the first place.

Identifying the Opportunities for Writer-Photographers

I always advocate that writers should analyse potential markets. Why waste your time writing a 2,000-word article, if the magazine uses nothing more than 1,200-word pieces? (If you want more advice on how to analyse a magazine for writing opportunities check out *The Complete Article Writer*, where I spend a whole chapter explaining this in more detail.) When analysing a magazine as a potential market, always look at the bylines (the writer's name/credit) accompanying each article and compare it with those names listed in the magazine's staff list. This is usually, though not always, near the front of the magazine. If all of the writers are named on the staff list it suggests that the opportunities for freelance writers are few and far between, whereas if the names do not appear on the staff list it suggests that this particular publication uses a lot of freelance material.

However, don't just look for the writer's byline: look for the photographer's byline too. This can be revealing.

Just like writers, photographers should be credited for their creative work too. However, magazines tend to take a different approach to this. Some will credit each photo individually. The photographer's credit might appear horizontally, directly underneath the photo, or it might be placed vertically, down one side of the photo. Occasionally, the photographer's credit will appear in a font size smaller than six somewhere close to the page's binding, which makes it difficult to find!

How photographers are credited can be influenced by how many different photographers' work has been used to illustrate a piece. If several photographers' images have been used, then the credit might appear next to each photograph, so it's clear which photographer took which photo. If the photography comes from just two sources, then the credit may appear near the start of the article (Photographs by Mr Smith and Mr Brown).

You may also see agency credits. This is where publications buy photos via a photographic agency (more in Chapter 8), and so these credits usually state the name of the agency (Alamy, Getty, Corbis), followed by the name of the photographer.

The way the words and photos are attributed in an article can indicate the opportunities that may or may not exist:

Words by John Smith. Photographs by Jane Brown.

This statement, usually found near the start of an article, tells the reader that one person wrote the words, whilst another person took the photographs. For writers who *don't* take photos this is good news because it clarifies that the magazine will try to find suitable images from other sources if the writer can't provide them. The editor is happy to buy the words from one person and buy photos from someone else.

Words and photographs by John Smith.

This credit tells the reader that the same person provided both the words and photos. If *every* credit in your target publication has this, that's a huge signal that this editor only uses writers who can provide the images too. Therefore, writers who don't take their own photos may find themselves unable to approach this market, whereas writers who do have a camera stand a better chance of breaking into this market. (There is one way around this, which we'll look at later in this chapter.)

So when you're analysing a publication, get into the habit of finding out who wrote the words and who took the photos, because this may identify markets that you hadn't considered before.

Analysing Images used by a Magazine

Writers are used to analysing a publication's articles to assess their style and format. We need to know how many words to write, whether to use complicated jargon for these readers, how long the sentences and paragraphs are, and whether articles are written in the first, second or third person. (Again, if you want more guidance on this, check out my *The Complete Article Writer*.)

It's also worth taking a look at the photographs, too, to see whether you can spot any stylistic clues in them.

Will your target publication use misty weather photos?

- Blue sky. One magazine I write for prefers blue sky photos. There's a reason for this. The editor wants the photograph to look inviting and to make the reader feel that they want to be there right now. Blue sky images are common in travel publications. Think about it. How many Caribbean Island travel articles have you seen that use foggy photos to illustrate the article? If you're writing an article that sells a destination, nothing beats a blue sky image. Don't become obsessed with blue skies, because whether an image needs a blue sky depends upon your publication's target readership and its subject matter. I've sold photos of foggy scenes and cloud-laden skies to magazines because their readerships are happy to go out in all weathers. An article about white water rafting probably won't mind using photos if it was raining when you took them. So, consider the weather conditions you see in the photos of your target publication.

- People. Some magazines make a stylistic decision about whether they want people in their photos or not. One editor recently issued guidelines clarifying that the front cover photo must now have someone in the image, preferably facing the camera. He doesn't want photos of people with their back to the camera staring out at an amazing view. He wants people looking towards the camera as if they are approaching the reader. Not all publications are as explicit as this, but you can often pick up general themes as you flick through the pages. If you spot that few photos, if any, have people in them, then that's a good sign that the editor prefers people-free photos. Are people posing, or are they captured acting naturally? What clothes and equipment are they wearing? (Think of your target readership. Subject-related publications will expect people in images to be properly equipped: walkers need to be in proper walking boots, not high heels; gardeners should be using a spade to dig a trench, not a saucepan from the cupboard under the sink; snorkelers should be using a proper snorkel, not the straw they were using to drink cocktails with; and cyclists and horse-riders should be wearing appropriate headgear.)

Are people in your images wearing the correct clothing or safety equipment?

- What size are the photos? Look at the size of the photos the magazine uses because this might indicate whether the publication can use your images. Generally, the glossier the publication the bigger they like using photos. A double-page spread is where one photo is used across both the left and right-hand pages. If you notice your target publication regularly uses images of this size then you need to ensure that your camera produces file sizes that are big enough to allow an editor to print your photos at this size. (As a rough guide, an A3 double-page spread is easier to produce from a camera with at least 17 megapixels.) Of course, this all depends upon the size of the magazine. An A5-sized magazine will require photos that can be printed (in landscape) at A4 size for a double-page spread, which only requires an 8-megapixel camera. Whilst some magazines might devote whole pages to photographs, they may use several images on a page, which means that each image is quite small. An A4 page of photographs containing four photographs means each image may be no bigger than six inches by four inches.

- White space. White space is an area of a photograph that has little or no detail. It is sometimes referred to as *negative*, or *open* space, because it offers editors an opportunity to use it for something else, such as the words in an article. Some of the best white space in a photograph is blue: blue sky! Any area with little detail can be used by an editor, so if you've taken a photograph of a person in the foreground who is in focus, but the background is blurred, the background might be perfect for some words from your article. It's worth looking to see how the editor of your target publication uses white space. You'll then know if it's worth submitting any suitable images you might have.

This image was used as a double-page spread, and the text of the article appeared in the sky.

Some editors will be grateful for any photographs that you can offer, but it's worth spending some time looking at the photo preferences of the editor, or picture editor, of your target magazine. It can affect payment. The rate of pay may depend upon the size of the image used, so if you spot your target publication likes using photos as large as possible and maximises the white space in them for the writer's text, it makes sense to offer them photos that meet these criteria.

Front Cover Images

Whilst you're scrutinising a magazine's images, don't forget to examine the most important photograph of all: the front cover image. Taking front cover photos is a skilled art, and some photographers specialise in this area, but there's no reason why one of the photos you're supplying with your article couldn't be ideal for this purpose. Bear in mind the following:

- Portrait. Generally, magazines use portrait images for the front covers, because of the magazine's shape when it's standing on the newsagent's shelf.
- White space. Some covers need a lot of white space.

They need space at the top for the magazine's masthead or title. Further white space is required to put teasing titles on the front to grab the reader's interest. Some magazines have a style where they use either the left or right-hand side of the image for these headlines.
- Focus. Look at where the main focus of the image is on the front cover. Is it in the centre, or is it to one side? Usually, the main focus of a front cover is a landmark, object, or the face (or head and shoulders) of an animal or person. Do you have any portrait-shaped images that fit this style?

Whenever I send a selection of images to an editor with my article, I always try to include at least one or two images that may also work as a front cover image. I didn't when I first started including photos with my submissions because it never crossed my mind at first. But one day an editor used one of the photos I'd sent to accompany my article as the front cover image, and I suddenly realised that I'd been missing a trick.

An expensive trick, you could say, because magazines pay for front cover images. It's something to think about, but consider your priority as selecting the best photos to illustrate your words.

Online Magazine Stores

Magazines have gone digital in the same way that books have. You can still buy print magazines in the shops and newsagents, but you can also buy digital versions to download to your tablet.

These services make magazine analysis so much easier, quicker and cheaper. There are several services around, but one I use is called *Readly*. (Search online for it to find the relevant link for your country of residence.) It's like *Netflix* but for magazines. I pay a flat monthly fee (equivalent to the cost of two average-priced magazines) and get access to the digital versions of the print magazines.

Not only can I read and access thousands of the latest issues of magazines from home and abroad (yes, you can access foreign publications too), it also gives me access to back issues. Sometimes a magazine makes two or three years' worth of publications available.

This makes it so much easier to get a stronger feel for a magazine's style. I can simply select a magazine's back issues and then over a dozen front covers appear on my screen. Immediately, I can spot front cover trends and styles for each publication.

Being able to look through back issues like this makes spotting stylistic choices much easier to identify. Swipe through several issues and you may establish that many publications are put together using a template. The same section of a magazine appears on the same page number in each issue. So, if you notice in one issue that the slot you're targeting begins with a double-page spread, check out the previous issues. If they all begin with a double-page spread photo then you know you need to supply images that meet this need.

It's also a great way to spot other trends, such as blue sky photos, and whether people appear in the images or not. And, not only that, but it will also clarify whether the magazine has a preference for using writer/photographers - those who can produce the complete words-and-picture package.

If you're keen to write for the magazine market, a subscription to a digital service like this is a sensible (and tax-deductible) investment.

Using Images to Secure a Commission

The ideal way to get your illustrated articles published is to secure a commission first. This is when you pitch an idea to an editor for a potential article, and they respond with a commission, instructing you to go ahead and deliver the piece by a deadline. Being commissioned like this is far more professional than writing on spec and submitting it with your fingers crossed, hoping that the editor might like it. Some magazines refuse to look at unsolicited submissions and will only deal with queries and pitches.

I've discovered that being able to offer an editor photos when I pitch an idea can help secure a commission. When I pitch an idea to an editor by email, I try to attach three or four example photographs to give them a flavour of the images I have available to illustrate my article. It's the sourcing of photos that takes time, so showing an editor I have photographs available means I'm offering them an easier life.

Looking through my records, I can tell you that my pitches where I offer photos are three times more likely to be commissioned than those where photos aren't included in my pitch.

Some of my regular magazine clients ask contributors for ideas on set themes, and they always ask for example images. This is why I argue that being a writer/photographer simply opens up more opportunities.

Here's an example of a pitch that worked:

Dear (Editor's name),

"We may be in the Welsh Borders, but our hills still provide a challenge!" - They're the words of one of the organisers of The

Long Mynd Hike - a 50-mile trek tackled during the first weekend in October within a 24-hour time limit.

The Long Mynd is in Shropshire, and it may only be 50 miles from the centre of Birmingham as the crow flies, but the Long Mynd Hike is a challenge relished by many walkers and hikers. There is over 8,000 feet of climbing, if you tot up all the hill climbs en route.

Would you be interested in an article of approximately 1800 words about the history of the Long Mynd Hike, its popularity, and the terrain involved, perhaps for your September or October issue? Many walkers and trekkers drive through Shropshire in search of the more majestic mountainous areas of Snowdonia and the Brecon Beacons, but they're missing out. For people who like a serious challenge, the Long Mynd Hike is a real test of the fittest. (The fastest completion time last year was 8 hours and 2 minutes!)

I have attached a couple of images here as an example of some of the photographs I have available, which may be suitable for illustration purposes. Thank you for your time. I look forward to hearing from you.

The editor liked the pitch, and the photos, and commissioned the article. You can read it online on my website at www.simonwhaley.co.uk/the-long-long-mynd-hike/

Using Someone Else's Photographs

It's possible to offer an illustrated article to an editor, even if you don't have a camera. The solution is to use someone else's photos, and, yes, it is possible to do this legally!

Although helping yourself to other people's photos from the Internet usually breaks copyright rules and means the image quality isn't good enough, the Internet can be a good source of image providers.

If you're writing about a destination, or organisation, who might benefit from the good publicity your article will generate, contact their public relations (PR) or media department. Seek out the organisation's website and search for PR or media contacts. They may be willing to help. Explain that you're writing an article and ask if they have any high-resolution photographs they can supply, which might be suitable to illustrate your article. (If you have a commission, mention this. It will add credibility to your request.)

Tourist attractions can be extremely helpful and might offer better photographs than you could take yourself, purely because they can stage the photograph better. I've written several features about the Royal Yacht Britannia, and the media contact there supplied me with an image of the royal yacht all decked out in her flags and with the various ensigns flying from the flagpoles. On the day I'd visited, none of the flags or ensigns were flying, so their images were better than anything I could offer the editor.

Occasionally, organisations commission aerial shots from photographers with drones. This gives them some amazing images they can use for publicity purposes, which they may be able to offer to you. And, unless you have a drone (and that's a whole new area of photography with its own set of regulations and laws), these images are photos that you simply cannot take yourself.

Always ask how the photographs should be credited. When you submit your work to your target editor, explain where you obtained the images from and how they should be credited, if the editor uses them. (Ideally, put this information in the file name of the image. See later in this chapter.) Include the contact name and details of the person you've been liaising with at the relevant media department. An editor may want to discuss whether they have any alternative images.

Some organisations have systems where you register with their media department and once approved this gives you access to their online media library of photographs. Always read the terms and conditions of the gallery to be sure that you are entitled to download and offer the images for publication use. Images available from these websites will be of high quality and suitable for publication. That's why they are there.

If an organisation requires payment for their photos never agree, commit, or make a payment. Firstly, if you're unsure whether your article will be accepted, you could be incurring expenditure you're unable to recover. Secondly, you don't know what your editor's budget is for buying photographs, let alone if they even have one.

In these situations, the best course of action is to give the editor all the necessary contact details for this image provider so that they can make the enquiries. Even if you haven't been able to provide photographs, the fact that you've given the editor details of where images may be found saves them so much time. You've still made their life easier.

Some media departments offer a handful of images for special events, which you can forward onto the editor when you submit your article. However, if you're invited to select images from a catalogue of hundreds of photos, it's best to give these contact details to the editor rather than try to select the photos that you think would illustrate your article best. Some publications have dedicated picture editors who are highly skilled at selecting images, so leave them to make the selection. Again, the fact that you've identified a suitable source of potential images means you've saved the editor time.

Finally, another way to use someone else's photographs is to team up with a photographer. This is particularly easy if your spouse, or partner, knows what to do with a camera, and using their images often negates any need to draw up contracts that stipulate how any payment for the illustrated feature should be split. Many husband and wife/life partner teams exist, where one takes the photos and the other provides the words.

Selecting the right Photos for your Articles

It's important to remember that, whilst an editor is always looking for photographs to accompany the written articles, editors want *relevant* photographs.

Whatever subject you're writing about, mention in your text items or objects that appear in the photographs you'll be submitting. When describing the atmosphere of a foreign market, for example, focus on one specific detail, which you know you've captured in your photographs. Perhaps there was a flamboyant market trader who drew large crowds to his stall. Or perhaps there was a moment when a local farmer walked his entire flock of sheep through the market, causing complete chaos. Think about ways you can tie your text and photos together.

Consider:

- Weather conditions. Are there elements of the weather you can mention, which your photos illustrate?
- Contrasts. Do you have photos of the same place from different seasons or different times of the day? Can you draw upon the contrast in these photos in your text? (This might encourage the editor to use both images.)

- Humour. Are there any humorous signs or situations you can highlight?
- Vistas. With photographs of views, mention things that can be seen from the view, which are visible in the photograph, and give details as to their size or distance.

Be sensible. Don't focus on the detail of something in every one of the 35 images you might offer to an editor. Be critical when selecting which images to include with your submission. Ask yourself how does this particular image help add more detail to your article? How is it relevant to this particular article? What does the reader lose by not seeing the photograph?

Tying the text and the photographs together like this encourages an editor to use your images. However, just because you've supplied the photographs doesn't make the editor duty-bound to use any of them. Some magazines pay per photo used, so the editor may be restricted by budget. However, the more photographs you can encourage an editor to use the better the financial reward might be.

Step-by-Step Articles

Step-by-step articles need photos. These articles show readers how to do something, usually in seven, eight or ten steps. You must think about each point in particular and decide how that point is best illustrated. In a step-by-step piece, the photograph should clarify any confusion that may arise if the reader were to rely solely upon the text. The photograph needs to show the reader how to undertake a particular action, or what something should look like when that step has been completed successfully.

A good way to write and illustrate a step-by-step piece is to undertake the exercise yourself, writing down every single step you take and photographing each and every step of the process. The challenge is to condense the numerous steps and photographs down to the key seven, eight or ten you need. Look at the process as a whole and identify the most difficult steps first, because these will be the steps where readers will rely on your visual clues. Then identify the key steps that link these difficult stages together. Don't forget to include a photograph of the finished item, so readers know what their efforts should look like.

Captions

Your photos must be captioned appropriately so the editor knows what the photo is of or whereabouts in the world it relates to. The best way to do this is to make the caption part of the photograph's filename when you save it. Getting captions correct is important. Readers will always write to the editor when they spot a mistake.

To determine what to mention in the caption, consider the six journalistic questions: *what, where, when, why, who* and *how*? You don't need to answer them all in every caption, but use them to guide you as to what information to include. If the photo contains action, describe it and explain why and where it's happening. If you've taken a photograph of two people judging entries in a best of breed category at a country show, you might caption it:

Two judges deliberating in the Herdwick Sheep Best of Breed category at the Westmorland County Show

That explains what is happening, who is involved, and where the event takes place. For some publications this would suffice, although others might require more specific detail, like so:

Mr Arthur Haltwhistle and Mrs Jane Ramsbottom judging the Herdwick Sheep Best of Breed category at the 20XX Westmorland County Show near Milnthorpe, Cumbria.

How much detail you give each caption will depend upon your target market. Check out the captions used to describe the photos in your target publication. Consider how much knowledge of the subject matter your target market might have. In the caption above I've identified that the Westmorland County Showground is near Milnthorpe in Cumbria. This may not be necessary for a Cumbrian-based publication but for a foreign-based publication, both Milnthorpe and Cumbria are vital pieces of information.

Unique References

Give each photo a unique reference in its filename, too. If you're offering an editor two similarly-captioned pictures, (perhaps one is portrait and one is landscape) you need something else to identify each image separately. The simplest solution is to use the file reference your camera gave your photo (although you don't have to).

When a photo is saved to a camera's memory card, it is usually given an incremental file number. The first photo you take might be saved as IMG-0001, the second as IMG-0002, and so on. That keeps you busy for the first 9,999 images, at which point some cameras start from IMG-0001 again. (Having two images in your photographic library with the same filename only causes a problem if you save them in the same folder/location. For most people this only causes difficulties if they take more than 10,000 photos in one day.)

Having a unique reference number and the caption as the photo's filename enables editors to correctly caption the photo, but if they have any queries, they can use your reference number to identify the specific photo in question when raising a query with you. My captions look like this:

IMG-0001 - Two judges deliberating in the Herdwick Sheep Best of Breed category at the Westmorland County Show - © Simon Whaley

Adding my name and the copyright symbol at the end of the caption clarifies to the editor that I took the photo and am the copyright holder. If I had obtained the photograph from another source I would put the copyright holder's information here.

At the End of your Document

At the end of my word processor document, after the main text of my article, I list all the filenames/captions of the images I'm supplying with the article. I use this as a checklist to ensure I've submitted all of the photographs I wanted to submit, and the editor can get an understanding of the type of images supplied, before even looking at them.

Never Insert Your Photos Into Your Text

Firstly, you're the writer/photographer, not the page-layout designer. Where you put your image probably isn't where the page-layout designer would dream of putting it. Page layout is a skill. Concentrate your efforts on your writing and photography skills.

Secondly, some word processor programmes reduce the quality of the image when embedding photos into text. They do this to keep the file size of your word processing document manageable. Photos embedded into text documents are rarely of a high enough quality to be used by the publication. If you insert photos into your text the publication won't be able to use them.

Submitting your Images

The days of posting articles in the physical post are long gone. Everything is submitted electronically these days, which means your photos need to be submitted electronically too. This can cause some problems, especially if you're sending numerous images. High-resolution photos have big file sizes.

Some email programmes limit the maximum file size of attachments. This might mean that the email becomes too big for your email programme to send. Alternatively, it could cause the editor problems at their end with their email system. It could cause confusion if you start splitting your photographic submission across half a dozen or more emails.

And some publications won't even open emails with attachments because of the potential threat of viruses.

If an editor asks you to submit your work electronically, ask them how they prefer photos to be submitted. Some magazines have a dedicated email address just for photographic submissions. The best solution I've found is to use an online storage website.

These allow you to save files/photos in an online folder. A useful benefit of these services is that they enable you to share documents and files with other users. All you have to do is create a folder on your online storage service and then upload your photographs from your computer to that online storage folder. Then you can select an option that creates a sharing link. This looks like a website address, and it only connects to this particular folder. All you have to do is paste this link in your email message to the editor.

When the editor receives your email, they click on the link and they're taken to the folder online, where they can easily download your images. There's no clogging up of email accounts, no crashing of connections, and some of these services even send you an email informing you when your folder has been accessed by someone. I find this particularly useful at offering me some reassurance that the editor has received my email safely.

Several of these services exist, and most offer some online storage for free. The amount of free storage ranges from two gigabytes up to fifty. I've found that a service offering two gigabytes is more than ample for this purpose. I simply create a folder for each article and once the article has been published, I delete it from the online storage service. That frees up space to be used in the future. And two gigabytes is ample space to hold folders containing images for dozens and dozens of my article submissions.

The following companies currently offer free storage space. All will happily charge you for extra storage space, but with a free account with each of these, that isn't necessary.

Dropbox: www.dropbox.com

Box: www.box.com

Microsoft's Skydrive: www.skydrive.com

If you have a Google account, you can share folders on your Google Drive, and Apple's iCloud service also allows something similar. So, the chances are, you already have one of these services, even if you don't use it.

There is another potential free service called WeTransfer (www.wetransfer.com)

WeTransfer is slightly different service in that you access it via your Internet browser, and then upload your images, add your email address and the address of to whom you want to send them along with a message. Agree to their terms and conditions and you can send up to 2Gb of files to any email address for free.

The recipient gets the email and, instead of the attachments, there is a link they can click on to download all of the photos. However, the downside to this service is that your recipient only has seven days to download the files. After that, the attachments are deleted. In most cases, this won't be a problem, but if your editor has just gone on their annual two-week holiday, they won't be back in time to download your attachments.

I have free accounts with all of these services, but I only use Box.com for my image submissions. I prefer to keep my article submissions separate from any personal folders. And, as I mentioned earlier, Box.com also emails me every time a shared folder is accessed. I'm sure other services can do this too if you explore their settings options.

Secondary Rights

I explained in Chapter 4 about the rights you grant to a magazine when they use your photos alongside your words. Ideally, *One Time Reproduction Rights* allows you to license the image to the magazine once, enabling you to offer that image to other publications to illustrate different articles.

This also allows you to use the photo again in different publishing opportunities, such as calendars or in books (or T-Shirts, mugs, whatever takes your fancy).

There are also what are known as *secondary rights*. Once your illustrated work has been published in a magazine or book, that document is available for photocopying. Several agencies around the world collect money paid out in recognition of these secondary rights and then distribute it to the rightful recipients. Here in the UK, we have two organisations: ALCS (Authors' Licensing and Collecting Society) and DACS (The Design and Artists Copyright Society).

They get their income from many sources, but perhaps the best example is that of photocopying. Educational establishments like schools, colleges and universities, pay a fee to the Copyright Licensing Agency in the UK (set up by ALCS and another organisation) that licences them to photocopy, or digitally scan, published material. If a university lecturer read your illustrated article and felt it would improve their students' understanding of a subject, the fee paid by the university to the CLA gives them the right to photocopy your article and distribute the copies to the students. Similar fees are collected from other large establishments like health authorities and government agencies. They also collect money from similar agencies around the world. The CLA then distributes this money to the distributing agencies (ALCS and DACS).

When you've had something published you should register that fact with at least one of these organisations. To do this you will need to know the ISSN (International Standard Serial Number) of the publication your illustrated piece appeared in. Many magazines print these (in small print) on the page where the editorial contact details appear in the magazine, although collecting agencies often have a database you can search to find this information.

Historically, the Authors' Licensing and Collecting Society (ALCS - www.alcs.co.uk) collected information about published words, and The Design and Artists Copyright Society (DACS - www.dacs.org.uk) collected information about published photographs. So when an illustrated article of mine had been published, I would log onto my ALCS account and register the article along with information about the publication it appeared in, the date of publication and the number of words my article contained.

Then, separately, I'd keep a spreadsheet logging the publication, ISSN, date of publication and how many of my photographs had been published alongside my words. I used this information to make an annual claim for the photographs from DACS. (DACS asks members to complete a claim form once a year, called Payback.)

While it was a little cumbersome, it was easy to remember: ALCS recorded the words, DACS recorded the photographs.

A few years ago, the system changed and ALCS allowed writers to claim for any photos published in their articles or books at the same time as they updated them with information about their published words.

It led to some confusion for some writer/photographers who became uncertain as to where they should record their photographs. If you're starting out, my advice would be to record everything through ALCS. ALCS can deal with photographs published in magazines and books at the same time as you register the words. That keeps everything nice and simple.

Because my photography markets have expanded, I continue to claim my words through ALCS and my photos through DACS. (DACS enables me to claim for TV usage, for example, which has happened, but ALCS can't - at the time of writing - take details of television usage.) What you can't do is claim your photos through ALCS and DACS! It's one or the other.

Once a year, these agencies distribute the income they've received to all writers and photographers. To be clear, payment does not mean that your article or photographs have been photocopied, merely that they're available for photocopying or scanning. But if your images have been published in a magazine or a book, then you are entitled to a share of that money.

These are called secondary rights because the writer/photographer has already licensed the primary rights directly to the magazine. To register for payments you need to join and become a member, for which there is a small, one-off charge, but this is deducted from your first payment, so there's no need to pay any money upfront. Once registered, you then need to give them details of every article you've had published, something that can be done online.

So if you successfully sell your illustrated article to a magazine, it means you can get paid twice, in effect. Once from the magazine, and then secondly from the secondary rights distributors. (And although I've mentioned it here in the chapter dealing with magazine articles, you can also record any images you have published in books, too.)

7

NON-FICTION BOOKS

If you enjoy writing articles on a specialised subject, or if you've undertaken a big personal project (such as a travel experience, or a change in your life), then you probably have enough material to write a book. Some of that material may include photographs.

Much of the information you've read so far relating to submitting photographs to magazines is as valid when writing a non-fiction book. There are, however, a few other points potential authors should consider.

Are Photos Necessary?

Yes, in a book about selling more of your words by offering photographs, I'm asking you whether photographs are necessary for your book.

Books containing photographs cost more to produce. They require different types of paper (generally more expensive), and a different (more expensive) printing process. Many illustrated books are published in parts of the world where production costs are lower.

When *Photography for Writers* was first published, it had no photographs. The publisher advised me that the additional printing costs made the book economically unviable. But printing methods have changed, and putting photos into both print books and ebooks is a little easier.

I've decided to include photos in the print book, even though they'll only appear in black and white because I still think you will gain something from being able to see those images. Colour photos would be lovely but that does make the book too expensive. (Although, if you're reading the ebook on a tablet you may see the images in colour.)

It doesn't matter whether you're planning a print book or an ebook, including photographs complicates the production process. It's not an insurmountable problem, based on the number of illustrated books that are published every year, but it alters the economics of the book. A publisher is always considering whether it's economically viable to publish the proposed book, and including photographs could be the element that tips the financial scales away from profitability.

Analysing the Market

There are, though, many books published every year that do include photographs, and my *Best Walks in the Welsh Borders* was one. I included photographs because I'd analysed the market. The book is a collection of 35 routes for walkers to follow, enabling them to explore the countryside around the English and Welsh borders. Most walking route books include photos because they tempt the reader to follow in the author's footsteps.

I looked at books produced by many publishers of walking guides and spotted that Frances Lincoln published a series called *Best Walks in* .... So I bought a couple of copies and analysed them. Each book had 35 routes of various lengths, and each walk was accompanied by two photographs. For my proposed book to fit into the series I had to offer photographs.

My proposal included copies of my illustrated published articles, to demonstrate my writing style and photography. I purposefully selected walking articles that had similar style photos to those used in their existing books.

Analyse similar books and assess the style of their photos. Will you need to provide wide vistas or close-up detail? Will you need to provide blue sky photos or images that are people-free? Do you need people in your photos? Don't forget to consider the size of the photos required. The images in *Best Walks in the Welsh Borders* were small because the book is small and designed to go in a jacket pocket. But if you're considering a coffee-table type book, the photos may need to be considerably larger. Is your camera capable of producing images of that size?

Plan the Images You Need

Always take more photos than you need. Whilst *Best Walks in the Welsh Borders* used, on average, two photos per walk, the publishers used a couple of other photos in other sections of the book. When I submitted my text and images, I supplied 8-10 photos per walk, giving the publishers a choice of images from which to select. We're back to my comment in the previous chapter that we're writer/photographers, not page layout designers. Publishers have a skill at understanding which images work best in books.

However, it's important to consider what photos you may need when you're planning your book because this might dictate how or when you take them:

- Local Customs and Events. A book about local customs or events will need you to go to these events and take photos on the days they take place. Will these take place on private property where you'll need permission? Obtaining the relevant permissions may take time, so the sooner you start arranging things, the better.

Plan in advance if you need to attend local events.

- Seasons. Are any of your images season-linked or might the season influence your image? Take a photo of your local high street in December and it may be festooned with Christmas decorations and coloured-lights. This is ideal for a Christmas subject, but perhaps best left until after the decorations have been removed if it isn't. Does having snow lying on the ground add to your image or is it inappropriate? Photos with people walking around in T-shirts and shorts might not be the best illustrations for your winter-themed book idea.

Are any of your images season-specific?

- Equipment and clothing. When writing about a specific subject matter and including people in your images, are they using the right equipment and wearing the correct safety clothing?
- Weather. Will your book inspire readers to go out and explore? If so, you should take photos on bright days, not gloomy, windswept days. Being reliant upon the weather causes planning issues, especially if you have to travel long distances. Travel flexibility helps immensely here, especially if you can stop working on one project to go off and take the photos you need for your book project.
- Plan routes to cut costs. Not all publishers offer advances, which means the first money you see from your book may be royalties on copies sold, some time (possibly a year or more) after publication. Any expenditure you incur whilst writing the book will be down to you. If you need photos from different

places, plan your route to reduce travelling time and expenditure.

- Up-to-date images. Do you already have some images in your photo library? Can you use these? Do they contain anything that dates the photo? Clearly-visible car registration plates date photos, as can car design. Has the landscape changed since you took the image? I've already mentioned how the iron bridge at Ironbridge has changed colour from grey to red. Further along the gorge at Ironbridge stands a power station, where there once stood four huge cooling towers. Last year, they were demolished and the landscape now looks completely different.

Out of date? The cooling towers of Ironbridge Power Station - now no longer in existence.

- Research. Before you travel, find out what you can about the area where you want to take photos. Search the Internet for images others have taken of the same places. What can you learn from them? What time of day are the better photos taken? Are they taken in the morning, afternoon, or evening? Do the photos look more dramatic taken during the day, when there are thousands of tourists about, or at the end of the day, when everyone has gone home? If visiting coastal areas, will your photos have more impact if the tide is in, or out? Do these images give you an idea about the best vantage points for taking these photos?

Writing a book takes time and ensuring you capture the photos you want for your book shouldn't be rushed either. Often, it is the photographs that grab the reader's attention when they first flick through a book. Seduce them with your photographs and they'll allow you to seduce them with your words.

Think Front Cover

The most vital photograph of all will be the one that goes on the front cover of your book. Readers will judge your book by its front cover, influencing whether they pick it up off the shelf or not. Despite it being your book, most publishing contracts state that the author will be consulted on the front cover image, but the publisher has the final say. Sometimes even the publisher doesn't have the final say, because large retailers can influence a book's cover. If they don't like it, they won't stock it, which is enough to make some publishers go away and have a rethink.

If offering your photographs to illustrate your book, then you might be able to influence the front cover choice to some extent, through the selection of photos you offer to the publisher. When selecting images, consider which of them would work well as a front cover.

- Is there an image in your collection that encapsulates the whole book? (If your book will be part of an existing series, what do you notice about the front covers of the other books in the series.) The front cover image needs to tell the reader what your book is about. If you're suggesting a region as a place to escape from the rat-race and relax, then your publisher may select an image that is calming, and people-free. If your book is about thrill-seeking adventures, the publisher might select a photo with lots of action in it.
- Book front covers are not as busy with text as magazine covers, because they only carry the book's title and author's name. This can influence how much white space is required for the front cover photo.
- Do you need just the front cover or an image suitable for the front, spine and back covers? Some books have a colourful front cover photo, but the spine and back cover are plain-coloured. For this arrangement, a portrait image works best. For wrap-around covers, where one image is used across the front, spine and back covers, a landscape-format image is better (although, the main subject of the photo will need to be on the right-hand side of the image to ensure it sits on the front cover of your book). If a back cover blurb is required, then there needs to be 'white space' on the left-hand side of the photo to allow for this. It's another reason for offering publishers similar images in portrait and landscape formats.

Mention to the publisher if there's a particular photo you like as a front cover, but don't expect them to use it. There may be many reasons why they can't. But offer them a selection of potential images and you stand a chance of getting something you like.

Captioning Images for Books

You should caption images for books in the same way that you would for a magazine: unique reference number, descriptive caption, followed by your name. Supply those images to the publisher as you would a magazine: submit the text as one document (without any photos embedded in the word processor document) and submit each photo as a high-resolution jpeg file.

However, because books are longer documents, there may be an additional requirement to suggest where a photo should be placed within a book. If your book is divided into chapters or sections, then adding this detail to the image's caption will be useful to the publisher, like so:

IMG-0001 - Chapter 1 - Two judges deliberating in the Herdwick Sheep Best of Breed category at the Westmorland County Show - by Simon Whaley

Whilst this doesn't tell the publisher exactly where the image should be placed, it clarifies in which chapter the image is intended to appear. A good copy-editor, or designer, will aim to place the picture as close to the specific reference of the subject matter in the text. Stipulating this information in the filename helps when supplying several hundred photos. You might also consider grouping photos together into separate folders for each chapter or section when saving them to an online storage folder.

List of Illustrations and Indexing Photos

Include a list of the illustrations and their captions at the end of your manuscript, similar to the list created at the end of a magazine article. Again, consider breaking this down into chapters.

When the publishing process is nearly complete, you'll be sent the page-layout proofs of your book. These will be an exact copy of how your book will look on the printed page, with your photos placed amongst your text. This is an exciting time, but don't get swept away in the emotion. Not only will your publisher require you to proofread your text, but you should also check the illustrations.

Are they correctly captioned? As the photographer, you know where the image was taken and what the image shows. During the production process, the publisher may change their minds several times about which photos they want to use and where. It's surprising how often a photo gets changed but they forget to change the caption.

Some publishers include a list of illustrations as part of the book. This usually appears at the front of the book, after the contents page but before the start of the main text. This list may comprise the caption and the page number it appears on. During the proofreading process, you need to check that the page number on this list is correct, and the right caption appears on that page number. Again, if an image is changed after this list has been created, this might be missed.

Depending upon your subject matter, your publisher may ask you to create an index. Enquire whether they require references to your photos to appear in your index. You may need to create two indexes: one for the words and one for the photos, which the publisher will then merge.

Self-Publishing

What I've said above relates mainly to traditional publishing, although most of it also applies to self-publishing. Even though it's possible to include images and photos in self-published books and ebooks, I would still recommend thinking carefully about whether you *really* need photos in your books.

For example, the Amazon platform charges a *delivery fee* when people buy your ebooks. The larger the file size of your book, the larger the fee. This will reduce the amount of profit you may make per copy. It depends upon the royalty rate option you choose, although many writers opt for the 70% royalty rate option. In this situation, the exact calculation Amazon applies is:

70% of the List price - delivery costs = royalty payment per book.

At the time of writing, Amazon charges UK authors 10p per megabyte. A text-only book may not even run to a file size of one megabyte.

Imagine your book is text only, and its file size is a tenth of a megabyte (about 100 kilobytes). You've opted for the 70% royalty rate and sell the ebook at £2.99. Your royalty will be calculated as follows:

£2.09 (70% of £2.99) minus delivery costs of £0.01 (a tenth of 10p) = royalty payment of £2.08.

However, a book with several photographs in it could extend to several megabytes. Imagine your ebook now had photos, which meant its file size now stood at ten megabytes. That now means your royalty rate has changed to:

£2.09 (70% of £2.99) minus delivery costs of £1 (ten megabytes at £0.10 per megabyte) = royalty payment of £1.09.

So those photos have reduced the royalty rate on every copy sold by 48%, or 99p.

Of course, you are still making a decent cut from that £2.99 list price, but the fact remains that the photos in the book have significantly impacted upon the profit you're going to make from each copy.

When it comes to print books, there's an additional cost if you want your photos printed in colour because you'll have to print on a different type of paper (one that can accept colour ink) and then there's the colour ink to take into consideration. As soon as you introduce colour the costs increase substantially.

And even if you decide to print images in black and white there is still a cost implication because photos take up space, which means your book will have more pages. This increases production costs.

So when it comes to illustrating your self-published book, do stop and carefully consider everything. Do you need to include *all* of the photos you'd like to include? Do you *need* to include any photos at all?

8

OTHER PHOTOGRAPHIC OPPORTUNITIES

Over time you may find your photographic library becomes substantial. Don't let those images languish in your library though. Send them out to work. Extra sales can generate a useful bonus income.

Photographic Agencies

Photographic agencies enable photographers to upload their photos to their agency database and sell them. Agency clients can include magazines, publishers, advertising agencies, and even individual people (even authors looking for the right image for their self-published book). Of course, agencies take a cut of the money they charge people to use your photos, and this varies from agency to agency. Some will pay the photographer as little as 10%, whilst others pay up to 50%. In recent years, the payments made to photographers has been squeezed and the agencies who used to pay 50% commission, now only pay between 20% and 30%.

Some agencies may pay a slightly higher commission rate if you sell your images through their agency exclusively. I sell my images through an agency called Alamy, to whom I've been contributing since 2009. Because I joined them soon after they established themselves and they are the only agency through whom I sell my photos, I'm still (currently) earning a commission rate of 50%.

Alamy wanted to cut the commission to 40%, but so many of their photographers complained (it should be remembered that without their photographers supplying images they have nothing to sell) and threatened to withdraw their images, Alamy made a concession. They agreed to retain a 50% commission rate if the photographer sold their images exclusively through them.

It took some further emails to clarify but going exclusive with them did not prevent me from selling my photos directly to magazines and publishers, which was my main concern. Any new photographers joining Alamy now will do so at a lower commission rate.

If you visit https://www.alamy.com/portfolio/simonwhaley you'll be able to see all of my images.

In addition to Alamy (www.alamy.com) there are other agencies you may wish to check out:

• Shutterstock (www.shutterstock.com)

• Adobe Stock (https://stock.adobe.com/uk/)

• istockphoto (www.istockphoto.com)

To find out more about supplying them with some of your photos, look for the *Sell Photos* or *Becoming a Contributor* links, which will give you much more information.

A word of warning: this is a numbers game, so don't expect to get rich. The downside to everyone being able to take publishable photos is that everyone is taking publishable photos. What was once the preserve of professional photographers is now accessible by anyone who can learn to take a good photo. Stock photography, as it is called, was once a lucrative income stream, with some photographers solely supplying photos to these sites. However, prices have dropped because so many people are doing this, and professional photographers can no longer survive financially solely by supplying photos to these agencies.

That's why I say look at these as a bonus. Since uploading some of my photos to Alamy, I've earned nearly $10,000, but I have thousands of photos on the website. National newspapers have bought my photos from here, book publishers have used my photos from this website to illustrate other books, and magazines have bought my photos from here. I've even had the search engine Bing buy one of my photos for use as a background image for their search website for one day. There's no way I would have been able to do that had I not been using an agency. I see it as a means of offering my photos to a wider audience.

If you like the idea of offering your photos to one or more of these websites, consider the following:

- Read the agency's terms and conditions. It'll clarify what their commission rate is of any sales you make, and when you'll be paid. Some agencies only release money when your account reaches a specific level.
- Check their submission process. All sites give detailed information about how big the file sizes need to be.
- Learn about their quality control. Some agencies are rigorous with the quality of images they accept for their site. You may need to send a test batch of images before you're accepted.
- If you are accepted as a supplier, think small and regular. Upload images in batches of ten. Once those

images have passed quality control you'll need to keyword them: give them accurate captions and give them keywords that searchers might use when looking for that sort of photo. Learning to keyword images can take time, but it gets quicker with practice.
- Search the agency websites for images similar to those that you have. If they don't have any of the subject matter you'd like to supply, then it might be worth submitting, but be sensible. Is your image of the Eiffel Tower any different to the other three million images the agency already has? However, if you have some different angles or different weather conditions than those on display, it means you have something to offer.
- Remember the law regarding photos. Images bought from these agencies are not just used for editorial purposes. You will need to clarify whether you have model or property releases for the photos you're uploading.

If you sell any photos, don't expect to be told who the customer was. Agencies act as middle-men and they make their money by taking a commission. I have, though, discovered some of my image sales, when I've turned a page in a magazine or newspaper. Exciting!

Tourist Brochures

Do you take photographs of places that are tourist destinations? If so, contact the relevant tourist authority and ask if they would be interested in seeing your images. Some authorities invite photographers to submit a selection of images, while others put your contact details onto their database and get in touch when they're putting together the next brochure. This system works well because it allows them to specify the type of images they're looking for, saving you from sending images that are of no interest to them.

Requests for images can vary from year to year, as tourist authorities try to attract different types of visitor to the area. One year they may be seeking quiet, rural landscapes, the next they might want photos of lots of people enjoying themselves at a food festival or market. Don't be dismayed if the tourist authority isn't interested in any of your images one year. Keep in touch, because their requirements will change from year to year. One year's request just might be for images that you happen to have.

Greetings Cards

This is a specialised market, but if you've captured the right sort of images, it's worth investigating. Do your market research. Look at greetings cards in card shops. In my experience, the independent stores and tourist shops, carry a better range of photographic greetings cards than the national chain stores. Spend an hour or so browsing the cards, looking at the style of photos and make a note of the manufacturers. Most have a company name and a website address on the back. The smaller greetings card companies are easier to approach than the multi-national companies, which is why an hour spent browsing your local independent greetings card shop can be better spent than an hour browsing on the Internet. When you've identified a list of potential card manufacturers, get in contact and ask:

- Do they consider freelance photographic submissions?
- How do they prefer to receive submissions: one or two images by email, or a selection of fifty uploaded to an online storage folder?

- What are their image requirements? (jpeg format, what particular image size)
- Are they looking for any particular subjects?

Don't expect to earn a fortune, but a sale of one image can be as much as the sale of an article to a small-circulation magazine.

Calendars

As with greetings cards, browse through calendar displays to make a note of who the publishers are and then contact them. That's how I first broke into the calendar market. A couple of the companies I came across had pages on their websites, specifically for photographers, stipulating the type of images they were currently looking for, and how they wanted them submitted. I knew I had a few possibilities in my library, so I put together a small batch and submitted them. They emailed, acknowledging my submission and said they'd be in touch if they were interested in any of them. Six months later they got in contact and bought five of my photos, paying me the equivalent of a good magazine commission. Since then, they've gone on to buy photos from me in most years.

Remember, when identifying potential calendar images, think about:

- Is it a photo you'd want to hang on your wall for up to 31 days at a time?
- What is it in the photo that tells you which month it is? Ideally, people should be able to tell what month it is (or at least the season) from looking at the photograph, not the date.
- Subject categories. If a calendar manufacturer seeks submissions for specific categories (dogs, national

parks, iconic landmarks, regional images, flora and fauna) you need to be clear which category your potential submission will fit.

Another bonus is that you often get given a copy, or two, of the calendar your image appears in.

Magazine Front Covers

You don't have to write an article to get your photos published in a magazine. Editors are always looking out for suitable front cover images. If you've captured an image that you think might be suitable for a magazine then get in touch with the picture editor (they're usually listed in the staff contact section of the magazine). Find out what their requirements are and if your image fits, send it in. Ideally, you should send in a small batch, rather than a single image. Don't expect an immediate response. Some picture editors will hold onto potential photos for use at any time in the future. Rates paid for front cover usage are higher than those for photos inside the magazine accompanying articles.

Some of the ideas suggested in this chapter might seem a world away from your original thought of taking a few photos to help you sell your words. But I wanted to include it because … you just never know. If you'd have told me ten years ago my photos would appear in national newspapers, in calendars and books and even on the Bing Search Engine home page, I've have said you were losing your mind. But it has happened.

Our photos are like our words. Once we've created them we have a library of material from which to draw. So why not exploit it, if we can?

Dora's Field near Rydal Mount, Cumbria. Selected for the Bing Search Engine homepage to mark the 250th anniversary of William Wordsworth's birthday.

9

PHOTOGRAPHY FOR RESEARCH

While the Internet has enabled writers to access information without having to travel to the next town, region or even another country, there are times when it's still necessary to leave the house and take your research out into the field. A camera can be extremely useful in these circumstances, and writers of both fiction and non-fiction can make use of the photographs they take.

Photography for Creative Writers

Think of your camera as a visual notebook. Instead of capturing words, you can record views, scenes, or funny moments. Scenes can evoke a mood or a sense of feeling within you. Capture it as a photograph and that image will help you re-establish that mood or feeling when it's time to write about it.

Get into the habit of taking photographs of anything and everything. You might also want to take images of the things you don't like, too: especially, if it evokes an emotional response. An image that stirs the emotions can do wonders for your creativity.

Perhaps the mannequin in the shop window is dressed in a style that would suit the main character in your story, or novel. Take a photo. Is there a house or a car that would be perfect for your antagonist? Take a photo. What would be your main character's favourite sweet or cake in a restaurant? When you see it, take a photo.

Learn to change your perspective with the camera. If you take a photo of a view, take another one from a different angle or perspective. Writing is all about looking at life and situations from a particular point of view. How many times have you written a short story and then rewritten the same story from a different character's perspective? The story can be quite different. The same goes for photographs. Take several images from different angles or perspectives and one might suddenly generate a new idea.

Traditionally, writers would print out photographs and then pin them to a noticeboard near their desk, or attach them to the wall. This still has merits, and if it works for you then do it. The modern equivalent of this mood board is the social networking site Pinterest (www.pinterest.com). This site allows you to upload photos onto different noticeboards. They're designed to be public, so other people who come across your images can copy them and pin them onto their own boards, but you don't have to have public boards. You can keep boards private, which means if you establish a board for each of your characters, you can upload your photos and use them to inspire you, knowing that no-one else can see them. Having online mood boards means you can access them wherever you have an Internet connection.

Copying Research Material

There are times when it's necessary to visit a library or a museum to see primary sources of information. Such research material cannot be borrowed, which either means taking a pen and notebook with you and making copious notes, or you could take your camera and photograph the material.

Before you travel, always enquire whether photography is permitted. In many cases it is, but with restrictions. Generally, photographing documents and images for your private, personal use is acceptable, and most research falls under this category. What you can't do (without permission) is share those photographs, or use them to illustrate your material in an article or book.

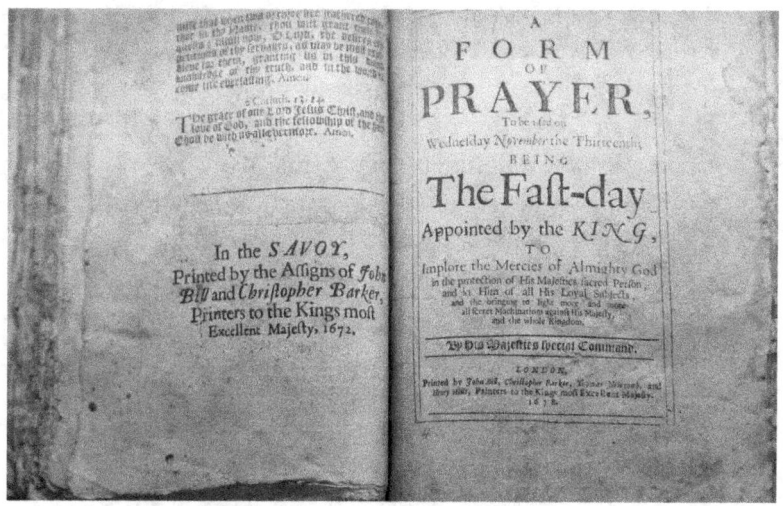

Photograph book pages to save you from taking hand-written notes.

- Set your camera to macro mode (the flower symbol) because this will improve your chances of taking photographs where the text is sharper.

- When photographing a book's page, lay the document as flat as you can. (Always abide by any rules regarding the handling of materials.) This will reduce any distortion of the text, or images, near the spine. You can now get apps for your mobile phone that are designed to take photographs of receipts and other expenses. However, they also work well for taking photographs of pages in books because they help to flatten the curve near the spine. This makes reading the text much easier.
- Hold your camera directly above the document, rather than at an angle, to ensure that as much of the image is in focus as possible.
- Consider the light source. If it's directly above it will cast a strong shadow (of your hands holding the camera) right onto the item you're photographing. Instead, position the document so the light source is from one side, rather than directly above.
- Do you need to turn off your camera's flash unit? Excess light can damage documents.
- Consider others. Turn off the *click* your camera makes when taking a photo. (In mobile and compact cameras these noises are electronic add-ons, not a result of the mechanical process of taking a photo.)
- Always take a photograph of the title, or cover page of any publication first, so you know the source of subsequent photos.
- Check your photo on the LCD screen. Have you captured what you need? Is it clear and readable? Zoom in to see how sharp it is. If it's not brilliant, take another one. Get it right now, whilst you have access to the documents.
- In low light conditions, and with the flash off, the camera will require longer shutter speeds. Hand-holding the camera increases the chances of blurring.

Switch on any Image Stabilising functions your camera has to help reduce this. If taking lots of images in these conditions, consider buying a small tripod.

When back at home, if you've photographed small amounts of text, type the information directly into your word processor. This will make searching the text at a later date easier. If you're capturing a lot of text data in photographic format, you can buy software that will import the photograph and then convert it into a fully-searchable and editable text document.

Don't just take photographs of text. Take photos of paintings, or other photos, particularly portraits, if you can get permission. Capture any official documents that might be of use to you, such as birth, marriage and death certificates, and even wills. If you're given access to private family letters, diaries or heirlooms, take photos. You won't remember everything about your trip. Taking a photograph can be more reliable than taking notes. You might not copy it correctly, however, a camera will always capture what it sees.

Capture unusual gravestones.

If you're out and about, perhaps photographing buildings, venues, views, or even gravestones, switch on your camera's geotagging facility if it has one. Geotagging uses satellite navigation to pinpoint where in the world you were standing when you took the photograph. It's surprisingly easy to forget where you were when you took a photo, and this resolves the problem brilliantly.

I always take photos of information panels now. Once you start looking for them you suddenly start noticing them everywhere. They're brilliant for basic facts about a place. It was during a commission to the Elan Valley reservoirs in mid-Wales that I spotted an information panel about its bouncing bomb connection. I took a photo of the information panel and then explored on foot and found the dam that Barnes Wallis had blown up. Amazingly, it still survives today, although it's a little bit more overgrown now. I took several photographs of it. I pitched an article to a magazine about the connection (timed to coincide with the anniversary of the Dambuster raids) and wondered if there were any historic images of the dam before Barnes Wallis blew it to smithereens. It was while reviewing my photo of the information panel that I saw the local authority's archives contact information listed. Perfect. One quick email to them and I had what I wanted. And all because I'd taken a photo of the information panel.

Finally, most cameras take videos, too. Sometimes a video works better than a photograph. You can take a batch of photos and then use software to create an image of the 360-degree view. But it's much simpler to take a video. Always check that venues are happy for you to take videos. Pan slowly, because this will make the image clearer when playing, and also help to retain some detail if you need to pause your video to scrutinise an element in the scene.

PHOTOGRAPHY FOR RESEARCH   141

Take photos of information panels. You can then refer back to them from the comfort of your desk.

Using your Photographic Library for Idea Generation

Your photographic library can be a brilliant idea generator. This visual stimulation can trigger memories, as well as spark off a whole series of ideas.

This is another reason why cataloguing software is useful. It all depends upon the keywords and caption data that you give your photos. This is why captioning is never time wasted. Whenever you're stuck for ideas, simply type a keyword into your cataloguing software and see which photos it retrieves. Scroll through the selection and see what you have. Is there a theme, or idea, that links a handful of these images together?

Whilst browsing through photos I'd taken on holiday, I realised I had several images of the inside of roofs (the weather hadn't been particularly good that week). I had photos of the intricately carved roof of a church, the roof of a modern glass structure and a thatched roof. From this, I created a travel article encouraging people to look up, when on holiday, which was published with those three photos providing the perfect illustrations.

This technique is also useful at presenting you with images throughout the seasons. If you regularly take photographs of your local viewpoint, for example, search for it in your catalogue. Perhaps you have four photos, one from each season, or twelve, one for each month of the year. There's your article idea: a year in the life of the view.

Keywords to think about include:

- Specific places: have you been to one place several times? Has it changed much over time? Having these *before* and *after* photos are a brilliant way of showing how things have changed. Nostalgic and local publications might be interested in these ideas.
- County/State: search for images taken in your local area. Are there any common themes? Can you create a tourist trail that might be of interest to a particular readership? Perhaps you have a collection of photos of great places to eat out, which might work for a food publication. Do you have any good photos of local gardens open to the public? Might you be able to interest a gardening magazine in a feature?
- Objects/Animals: When I had a dog, I discovered she liked being in many of my photos. I included her name in the caption data and when I searched for it I was a little surprised at the number of photos the cataloguing system returned. It gave me an idea for an article though: how to be the perfect dog owner. This piece had twenty tips and was accompanied by twenty photos illustrating each tip.

Of course, the search terms you'll use will depend upon the type of photos you take and the caption data you give each photo. But even if you don't have any cataloguing software, simply spending a few minutes opening each folder of photos on your computer and scrolling through what you have can help generate thoughts and ideas. It's surprising what you forget.

It's another reason why I use the Google Photos app now. It reminds me of what I was doing (or rather, what I was taking photos of) one year, two years, three years, etc ago. After the initial shock of *that was never six years ago*, the memories come flooding back and suddenly the magazine article ideas start pinging in my head.

10

THE FINAL EXPOSURE

They say old photographers never die, they simply go out of focus. However, the fact remains that our final exposure will arrive one day and, just like we must with our writing assets, we should also consider what happens to our photographic assets after our death.

Thanks to copyright laws, our photos can continue to live and generate an income for another 70 years after our demise. This *afterlife* needs a little preparation before we compose our final frame.

In the UK alone, it is estimated that two-thirds of the population do not have a will, and of those who do, who knows how many have made specific mention of their photographs in their final instructions. Even if none of your images has been published before your death, they're still an asset that could be exploited commercially by your beneficiaries.

When it comes to leaving items in our wills, photographers often think of physical assets, such as camera bodies, lenses, and possibly those boxes of 35mm transparencies that are stuck up in the loft and haven't seen daylight since the 20th century. But it's important to remember that all the images we create, including the digital ones, are assets that can be bequeathed.

As long as we retain the copyright in our images, we can bequeath this to whom we like in our will. And because the copyright can be exploited for 70 years after our death, any income generated from it could potentially benefit two generations. If you're going to leave the copyright to your child, you could well be passing on an asset that they can bequeath in their own will too. Therefore, you must talk to your beneficiaries, so they understand exactly what you are leaving them.

Understanding the Options

When I sat down with my solicitor to sort out my first will, I assumed all I needed was to have a clause stating whom I was leaving the copyright to. For some people, a simple statement like this is sufficient. The simplest option is to leave everything (copyright and the actual images) to one person, or beneficiary (such as a museum, or charity). But there are other options.

You could bequeath the copyright in the images to one person and leave any income generated from images you may have uploaded to a photographic agency account to someone else. For example, if your agency account generates an income of £500 per year, you could bequeath the copyright in the images to your children, and the income from the agency account to your surviving partner. Your children could still exploit the other rights in your images as well as any other of your images that are not on the agency website, and they would benefit from the income this produces, but any income generated through the agency alone would be paid directly to your surviving partner. Your partner can then choose to bequeath this income to anyone they like in their own will.

Other Points to Consider

It's important to think of all income sources that your photos generate. If your images have been published in books, magazines, or on television, then you might be entitled to secondary rights income, such as those collected via the Design & Artists Copyright Service, DACS (www.dacs.org.uk), which can be accessed via their Payback scheme. You're entitled to any monies collected during your lifetime, but again, the copyright holder can continue to claim this money after your death, as long they can prove they hold the copyright in your photos.

This also means you must keep accurate records of the rights you're selling in your photographs, especially those where you assign copyright. Will your beneficiary know which rights are available in each of your images? Remember, new rights may be created after your demise.

Spend time thinking about who you would like to benefit from your photographic efforts when you're gone. Everyone's circumstances are different, so the best course of action is to get a solicitor to draw up your will. Avoid the do-it-yourself forms from stationers, this is not the time to do this on the cheap. My professionally-drawn up will was relatively straightforward and cost me £100. The solicitor also clarified many issues for me, as well as pointing out things I hadn't thought of. For example, some photographers might want to leave their copyright to grandchildren. That's fine, but if you died tomorrow, and your grandchild is only 8 years old, who's going to administer the copyright until they're 18 and can legally enter contracts in their name?

Thinking about our death is something we'd much rather push to the back of our minds. But, we're creators. We create words and now, with the help of this book, I hope you'll be creating photos too. Our words and our pictures are content - material that can be licensed, thanks to the protection that copyright gives us. It is worth spending an afternoon thinking about how you'd like your creations to be distributed, and to whom, after you've gone.

The most important thing is to leave clear instructions, which is why a will is important. It will make your beneficiaries lives' easier if you've thought about it beforehand.

Smile!

So there we have it. I hope this book has given you ideas, and some confidence, about how having a camera can help you to develop your writing further. Just because you don't have four different camera bodies and 22 interchangeable lenses, that doesn't mean your photos are any less publishable. As the saying goes, the best camera is the one you have in your hands: better that one, than none at all.

Go on. Be brave! Whip out your camera and start taking photos. Photography is like writing, you know. The more you do it, the better at it you become.

Be realistic. Don't expect your first photo to be selected for the front cover of *Time* magazine. Start small. Send in photos to the letter pages of magazines, and then try using some of your images to illustrate your articles. Who knows? In a few years you may even be taking photographs for your own illustrated book.

Good luck.

Click!

ENJOYED THE BOOK?

I hope you enjoyed the book. If you have, then I would be most grateful if you could spend a couple of moments leaving a review on the site you bought this from.
Thank you very much.

Simon

ALSO BY SIMON WHALEY

Also in the Practical Writer Series:

The Complete Article Writer

The Positively Productive Writer (Second Edition)

Other Books:

One Hundred Ways For A Dog To Train Its Human

One Hundred Muddy Paws For Thought

Puppytalk: 50 Ways To Make Friends With Your Puppy

Fundraising For A Community Project

Best Walks in the Welsh Borders

The Little Book of Alternative Garden Wisdom

The Bluffer's Guide to Hiking

The Bluffer's Guide to Dogs

Running A Writers' Circle

The Bluffer's Guide to Banking

The Business of Writing - Volume 1

The Business of Writing - Volume 2

The Business of Writing - Volume 3

Contributed To:

The Freelance Photographer's Project Book

100 Greatest Walks in Britain

100 Stories For Queensland

ABOUT THE AUTHOR

Simon Whaley is a freelance writer, author and photographer. He's the bestselling author of *One Hundred Ways For A Dog To Train Its Human*, published by Hodder & Stoughton in print and eBook format. When first published, it spent December 2003 on the UK bestseller lists, and it has also been published in North America, Portugal, Italy and Iceland.

His articles have appeared in publications as diverse as the Daily Express, the Observer, Cheshire Life, The Lady, BBC Countryfile, British Heritage, The People's Friend, Country Walking, and Outdoor Photography.

His short stories have been published in Woman's Weekly Fiction Special, Take a Break, Take a Break's Fiction Feast, The Weekly News, Ireland's Own, The People's Friend and That's Life Fast Fiction (Australia).

To Connect With Simon:
www.simonwhaley.co.uk
contact@simonwhaley.co.uk

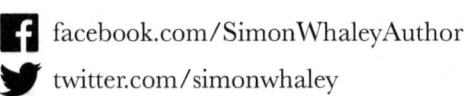

facebook.com/SimonWhaleyAuthor
twitter.com/simonwhaley

www.ingramcontent.com/pod-product-compliance
Lightning Source LLC
Chambersburg PA
CBHW071630080526
44588CB00010B/1348